C-659   CAREER EXAMINATION SERIES

This is your
PASSBOOK for...

Principal File Clerk

Test Preparation Study Guide
Questions & Answers

COPYRIGHT NOTICE

This book is SOLELY intended for, is sold ONLY to, and its use is RESTRICTED to individual, bona fide applicants or candidates who qualify by virtue of having seriously filed applications for appropriate license, certificate, professional and/or promotional advancement, higher school matriculation, scholarship, or other legitimate requirements of education and/or governmental authorities.

This book is NOT intended for use, class instruction, tutoring, training, duplication, copying, reprinting, excerption, or adaptation, etc., by:

1) Other publishers
2) Proprietors and/or Instructors of "Coaching" and/or Preparatory Courses
3) Personnel and/or Training Divisions of commercial, industrial, and governmental organizations
4) Schools, colleges, or universities and/or their departments and staffs, including teachers and other personnel
5) Testing Agencies or Bureaus
6) Study groups which seek by the purchase of a single volume to copy and/or duplicate and/or adapt this material for use by the group as a whole without having purchased individual volumes for each of the members of the group
7) Et al.

Such persons would be in violation of appropriate Federal and State statutes.

PROVISION OF LICENSING AGREEMENTS – Recognized educational, commercial, industrial, and governmental institutions and organizations, and others legitimately engaged in educational pursuits, including training, testing, and measurement activities, may address request for a licensing agreement to the copyright owners, who will determine whether, and under what conditions, including fees and charges, the materials in this book may be used them. In other words, a licensing facility exists for the legitimate use of the material in this book on other than an individual basis. However, it is asseverated and affirmed here that the material in this book CANNOT be used without the receipt of the express permission of such a licensing agreement from the Publishers. Inquiries re licensing should be addressed to the company, attention rights and permissions department.

All rights reserved, including the right of reproduction in whole or in part, in any form or by any means, electronic or mechanical, including photocopying, recording, or by any information storage and retrieval system, without permission in writing from the Publisher.

Copyright © 2025 by
National Learning Corporation

212 Michael Drive, Syosset, NY 11791
(516) 921-8888 • www.passbooks.com
E-mail: info@passbooks.com

PASSBOOK® SERIES

THE *PASSBOOK® SERIES* has been created to prepare applicants and candidates for the ultimate academic battlefield – the examination room.

At some time in our lives, each and every one of us may be required to take an examination – for validation, matriculation, admission, qualification, registration, certification, or licensure.

Based on the assumption that every applicant or candidate has met the basic formal educational standards, has taken the required number of courses, and read the necessary texts, the *PASSBOOK® SERIES* furnishes the one special preparation which may assure passing with confidence, instead of failing with insecurity. Examination questions – together with answers – are furnished as the basic vehicle for study so that the mysteries of the examination and its compounding difficulties may be eliminated or diminished by a sure method.

This book is meant to help you pass your examination provided that you qualify and are serious in your objective.

The entire field is reviewed through the huge store of content information which is succinctly presented through a provocative and challenging approach – the question-and-answer method.

A climate of success is established by furnishing the correct answers at the end of each test.

You soon learn to recognize types of questions, forms of questions, and patterns of questioning. You may even begin to anticipate expected outcomes.

You perceive that many questions are repeated or adapted so that you can gain acute insights, which may enable you to score many sure points.

You learn how to confront new questions, or types of questions, and to attack them confidently and work out the correct answers.

You note objectives and emphases, and recognize pitfalls and dangers, so that you may make positive educational adjustments.

Moreover, you are kept fully informed in relation to new concepts, methods, practices, and directions in the field.

You discover that you are actually taking the examination all the time: you are preparing for the examination by "taking" an examination, not by reading extraneous and/or supererogatory textbooks.

In short, this PASSBOOK®, used directedly, should be an important factor in helping you to pass your test.

PRINCIPAL FILE CLERK

DUTIES
As Principal File Clerk you would supervise a program of systematic storage, reference, and disposition of agency records, monitoring all files activities for accuracy and adherence to specified procedure. You would maintain satisfactory production levels; insure that schedules are met and various program areas are properly serviced; and you might revise and devise files procedures as necessary. You would supervise an extremely large clerical staff of varying levels and provide assistance and guidance to staff in filing practices and in interpreting agency policy and procedures relating to the filing function.

SCOPE OF THE EXAMINATION
The multiple-choice written test will cover knowledge, skills, and/or abilities in such areas as:
1. Filing practices, indexing, soning and cross-referencing; filing equipment and terminology;
2. Clerical abilities;
3. Understanding and interpreting written material;
4. Office management; and
5. Administrative supervision.

HOW TO TAKE A TEST

I. YOU MUST PASS AN EXAMINATION

A. *WHAT EVERY CANDIDATE SHOULD KNOW*

Examination applicants often ask us for help in preparing for the written test. What can I study in advance? What kinds of questions will be asked? How will the test be given? How will the papers be graded?

As an applicant for a civil service examination, you may be wondering about some of these things. Our purpose here is to suggest effective methods of advance study and to describe civil service examinations.

Your chances for success on this examination can be increased if you know how to prepare. Those "pre-examination jitters" can be reduced if you know what to expect. You can even experience an adventure in good citizenship if you know why civil service exams are given.

B. *WHY ARE CIVIL SERVICE EXAMINATIONS GIVEN?*

Civil service examinations are important to you in two ways. As a citizen, you want public jobs filled by employees who know how to do their work. As a job seeker, you want a fair chance to compete for that job on an equal footing with other candidates. The best-known means of accomplishing this two-fold goal is the competitive examination.

Exams are widely publicized throughout the nation. They may be administered for jobs in federal, state, city, municipal, town or village governments or agencies.

Any citizen may apply, with some limitations, such as the age or residence of applicants. Your experience and education may be reviewed to see whether you meet the requirements for the particular examination. When these requirements exist, they are reasonable and applied consistently to all applicants. Thus, a competitive examination may cause you some uneasiness now, but it is your privilege and safeguard.

C. *HOW ARE CIVIL SERVICE EXAMS DEVELOPED?*

Examinations are carefully written by trained technicians who are specialists in the field known as "psychological measurement," in consultation with recognized authorities in the field of work that the test will cover. These experts recommend the subject matter areas or skills to be tested; only those knowledges or skills important to your success on the job are included. The most reliable books and source materials available are used as references. Together, the experts and technicians judge the difficulty level of the questions.

Test technicians know how to phrase questions so that the problem is clearly stated. Their ethics do not permit "trick" or "catch" questions. Questions may have been tried out on sample groups, or subjected to statistical analysis, to determine their usefulness.

Written tests are often used in combination with performance tests, ratings of training and experience, and oral interviews. All of these measures combine to form the best-known means of finding the right person for the right job.

II. HOW TO PASS THE WRITTEN TEST

A. NATURE OF THE EXAMINATION

To prepare intelligently for civil service examinations, you should know how they differ from school examinations you have taken. In school you were assigned certain definite pages to read or subjects to cover. The examination questions were quite detailed and usually emphasized memory. Civil service exams, on the other hand, try to discover your present ability to perform the duties of a position, plus your potentiality to learn these duties. In other words, a civil service exam attempts to predict how successful you will be. Questions cover such a broad area that they cannot be as minute and detailed as school exam questions.

In the public service similar kinds of work, or positions, are grouped together in one "class." This process is known as *position-classification*. All the positions in a class are paid according to the salary range for that class. One class title covers all of these positions, and they are all tested by the same examination.

B. FOUR BASIC STEPS

1) Study the announcement

How, then, can you know what subjects to study? Our best answer is: "Learn as much as possible about the class of positions for which you've applied." The exam will test the knowledge, skills and abilities needed to do the work.

Your most valuable source of information about the position you want is the official exam announcement. This announcement lists the training and experience qualifications. Check these standards and apply only if you come reasonably close to meeting them.

The brief description of the position in the examination announcement offers some clues to the subjects which will be tested. Think about the job itself. Review the duties in your mind. Can you perform them, or are there some in which you are rusty? Fill in the blank spots in your preparation.

Many jurisdictions preview the written test in the exam announcement by including a section called "Knowledge and Abilities Required," "Scope of the Examination," or some similar heading. Here you will find out specifically what fields will be tested.

2) Review your own background

Once you learn in general what the position is all about, and what you need to know to do the work, ask yourself which subjects you already know fairly well and which need improvement. You may wonder whether to concentrate on improving your strong areas or on building some background in your fields of weakness. When the announcement has specified "some knowledge" or "considerable knowledge," or has used adjectives like "beginning principles of…" or "advanced … methods," you can get a clue as to the number and difficulty of questions to be asked in any given field. More questions, and hence broader coverage, would be included for those subjects which are more important in the work. Now weigh your strengths and weaknesses against the job requirements and prepare accordingly.

3) Determine the level of the position

Another way to tell how intensively you should prepare is to understand the level of the job for which you are applying. Is it the entering level? In other words, is this the position in which beginners in a field of work are hired? Or is it an intermediate or advanced level? Sometimes this is indicated by such words as "Junior" or "Senior" in the class title. Other jurisdictions use Roman numerals to designate the level – Clerk I, Clerk II, for example. The word "Supervisor" sometimes appears in the title. If the level is not indicated by the title, check the description of duties. Will you be working under very close supervision, or will you have responsibility for independent decisions in this work?

4) Choose appropriate study materials

Now that you know the subjects to be examined and the relative amount of each subject to be covered, you can choose suitable study materials. For beginning level jobs, or even advanced ones, if you have a pronounced weakness in some aspect of your training, read a modern, standard textbook in that field. Be sure it is up to date and has general coverage. Such books are normally available at your library, and the librarian will be glad to help you locate one. For entry-level positions, questions of appropriate difficulty are chosen – neither highly advanced questions, nor those too simple. Such questions require careful thought but not advanced training.

If the position for which you are applying is technical or advanced, you will read more advanced, specialized material. If you are already familiar with the basic principles of your field, elementary textbooks would waste your time. Concentrate on advanced textbooks and technical periodicals. Think through the concepts and review difficult problems in your field.

These are all general sources. You can get more ideas on your own initiative, following these leads. For example, training manuals and publications of the government agency which employs workers in your field can be useful, particularly for technical and professional positions. A letter or visit to the government department involved may result in more specific study suggestions, and certainly will provide you with a more definite idea of the exact nature of the position you are seeking.

III. KINDS OF TESTS

Tests are used for purposes other than measuring knowledge and ability to perform specified duties. For some positions, it is equally important to test ability to make adjustments to new situations or to profit from training. In others, basic mental abilities not dependent on information are essential. Questions which test these things may not appear as pertinent to the duties of the position as those which test for knowledge and information. Yet they are often highly important parts of a fair examination. For very general questions, it is almost impossible to help you direct your study efforts. What we can do is to point out some of the more common of these general abilities needed in public service positions and describe some typical questions.

1) General information

Broad, general information has been found useful for predicting job success in some kinds of work. This is tested in a variety of ways, from vocabulary lists to questions about current events. Basic background in some field of work, such as sociology or economics, may be sampled in a group of questions. Often these are principles which have become familiar to most persons through exposure rather than through formal training. It is difficult to advise you how to study for these questions; being alert to the world around you is our best suggestion.

2) Verbal ability

An example of an ability needed in many positions is verbal or language ability. Verbal ability is, in brief, the ability to use and understand words. Vocabulary and grammar tests are typical measures of this ability. Reading comprehension or paragraph interpretation questions are common in many kinds of civil service tests. You are given a paragraph of written material and asked to find its central meaning.

3) Numerical ability

Number skills can be tested by the familiar arithmetic problem, by checking paired lists of numbers to see which are alike and which are different, or by interpreting charts and graphs. In the latter test, a graph may be printed in the test booklet which you are asked to use as the basis for answering questions.

4) Observation

A popular test for law-enforcement positions is the observation test. A picture is shown to you for several minutes, then taken away. Questions about the picture test your ability to observe both details and larger elements.

5) Following directions

In many positions in the public service, the employee must be able to carry out written instructions dependably and accurately. You may be given a chart with several columns, each column listing a variety of information. The questions require you to carry out directions involving the information given in the chart.

6) Skills and aptitudes

Performance tests effectively measure some manual skills and aptitudes. When the skill is one in which you are trained, such as typing or shorthand, you can practice. These tests are often very much like those given in business school or high school courses. For many of the other skills and aptitudes, however, no short-time preparation can be made. Skills and abilities natural to you or that you have developed throughout your lifetime are being tested.

Many of the general questions just described provide all the data needed to answer the questions and ask you to use your reasoning ability to find the answers. Your best preparation for these tests, as well as for tests of facts and ideas, is to be at your physical and mental best. You, no doubt, have your own methods of getting into an exam-taking mood and keeping "in shape." The next section lists some ideas on this subject.

IV. KINDS OF QUESTIONS

Only rarely is the "essay" question, which you answer in narrative form, used in civil service tests. Civil service tests are usually of the short-answer type. Full instructions for answering these questions will be given to you at the examination. But in case this is your first experience with short-answer questions and separate answer sheets, here is what you need to know:

1) Multiple-choice Questions

Most popular of the short-answer questions is the "multiple choice" or "best answer" question. It can be used, for example, to test for factual knowledge, ability to solve problems or judgment in meeting situations found at work.

A multiple-choice question is normally one of three types—
- It can begin with an incomplete statement followed by several possible endings. You are to find the one ending which *best* completes the statement, although some of the others may not be entirely wrong.
- It can also be a complete statement in the form of a question which is answered by choosing one of the statements listed.

- It can be in the form of a problem – again you select the best answer.

Here is an example of a multiple-choice question with a discussion which should give you some clues as to the method for choosing the right answer:

When an employee has a complaint about his assignment, the action which will *best* help him overcome his difficulty is to
A. discuss his difficulty with his coworkers
B. take the problem to the head of the organization
C. take the problem to the person who gave him the assignment
D. say nothing to anyone about his complaint

In answering this question, you should study each of the choices to find which is best. Consider choice "A" – Certainly an employee may discuss his complaint with fellow employees, but no change or improvement can result, and the complaint remains unresolved. Choice "B" is a poor choice since the head of the organization probably does not know what assignment you have been given, and taking your problem to him is known as "going over the head" of the supervisor. The supervisor, or person who made the assignment, is the person who can clarify it or correct any injustice. Choice "C" is, therefore, correct. To say nothing, as in choice "D," is unwise. Supervisors have and interest in knowing the problems employees are facing, and the employee is seeking a solution to his problem.

2) True/False Questions

The "true/false" or "right/wrong" form of question is sometimes used. Here a complete statement is given. Your job is to decide whether the statement is right or wrong.

SAMPLE: A roaming cell-phone call to a nearby city costs less than a non-roaming call to a distant city.

This statement is wrong, or false, since roaming calls are more expensive.

This is not a complete list of all possible question forms, although most of the others are variations of these common types. You will always get complete directions for answering questions. Be sure you understand *how* to mark your answers – ask questions until you do.

V. RECORDING YOUR ANSWERS

Computer terminals are used more and more today for many different kinds of exams.

For an examination with very few applicants, you may be told to record your answers in the test booklet itself. Separate answer sheets are much more common. If this separate answer sheet is to be scored by machine – and this is often the case – it is highly important that you mark your answers correctly in order to get credit.

An electronic scoring machine is often used in civil service offices because of the speed with which papers can be scored. Machine-scored answer sheets must be marked with a pencil, which will be given to you. This pencil has a high graphite content which responds to the electronic scoring machine. As a matter of fact, stray dots may register as answers, so do not let your pencil rest on the answer sheet while you are pondering the correct answer. Also, if your pencil lead breaks or is otherwise defective, ask for another.

Since the answer sheet will be dropped in a slot in the scoring machine, be careful not to bend the corners or get the paper crumpled.

The answer sheet normally has five vertical columns of numbers, with 30 numbers to a column. These numbers correspond to the question numbers in your test booklet. After each number, going across the page are four or five pairs of dotted lines. These short dotted lines have small letters or numbers above them. The first two pairs may also have a "T" or "F" above the letters. This indicates that the first two pairs only are to be used if the questions are of the true-false type. If the questions are multiple choice, disregard the "T" and "F" and pay attention only to the small letters or numbers.

Answer your questions in the manner of the sample that follows:

32. The largest city in the United States is
    A. Washington, D.C.
    B. New York City
    C. Chicago
    D. Detroit
    E. San Francisco

1) Choose the answer you think is best. (New York City is the largest, so "B" is correct.)
2) Find the row of dotted lines numbered the same as the question you are answering. (Find row number 32)
3) Find the pair of dotted lines corresponding to the answer. (Find the pair of lines under the mark "B.")
4) Make a solid black mark between the dotted lines.

VI. BEFORE THE TEST

Common sense will help you find procedures to follow to get ready for an examination. Too many of us, however, overlook these sensible measures. Indeed, nervousness and fatigue have been found to be the most serious reasons why applicants fail to do their best on civil service tests. Here is a list of reminders:

- Begin your preparation early – Don't wait until the last minute to go scurrying around for books and materials or to find out what the position is all about.
- Prepare continuously – An hour a night for a week is better than an all-night cram session. This has been definitely established. What is more, a night a week for a month will return better dividends than crowding your study into a shorter period of time.
- Locate the place of the exam – You have been sent a notice telling you when and where to report for the examination. If the location is in a different town or otherwise unfamiliar to you, it would be well to inquire the best route and learn something about the building.
- Relax the night before the test – Allow your mind to rest. Do not study at all that night. Plan some mild recreation or diversion; then go to bed early and get a good night's sleep.
- Get up early enough to make a leisurely trip to the place for the test – This way unforeseen events, traffic snarls, unfamiliar buildings, etc. will not upset you.
- Dress comfortably – A written test is not a fashion show. You will be known by number and not by name, so wear something comfortable.

- Leave excess paraphernalia at home – Shopping bags and odd bundles will get in your way. You need bring only the items mentioned in the official notice you received; usually everything you need is provided. Do not bring reference books to the exam. They will only confuse those last minutes and be taken away from you when in the test room.
- Arrive somewhat ahead of time – If because of transportation schedules you must get there very early, bring a newspaper or magazine to take your mind off yourself while waiting.
- Locate the examination room – When you have found the proper room, you will be directed to the seat or part of the room where you will sit. Sometimes you are given a sheet of instructions to read while you are waiting. Do not fill out any forms until you are told to do so; just read them and be prepared.
- Relax and prepare to listen to the instructions
- If you have any physical problem that may keep you from doing your best, be sure to tell the test administrator. If you are sick or in poor health, you really cannot do your best on the exam. You can come back and take the test some other time.

VII. AT THE TEST

The day of the test is here and you have the test booklet in your hand. The temptation to get going is very strong. Caution! There is more to success than knowing the right answers. You must know how to identify your papers and understand variations in the type of short-answer question used in this particular examination. Follow these suggestions for maximum results from your efforts:

1) Cooperate with the monitor

The test administrator has a duty to create a situation in which you can be as much at ease as possible. He will give instructions, tell you when to begin, check to see that you are marking your answer sheet correctly, and so on. He is not there to guard you, although he will see that your competitors do not take unfair advantage. He wants to help you do your best.

2) Listen to all instructions

Don't jump the gun! Wait until you understand all directions. In most civil service tests you get more time than you need to answer the questions. So don't be in a hurry. Read each word of instructions until you clearly understand the meaning. Study the examples, listen to all announcements and follow directions. Ask questions if you do not understand what to do.

3) Identify your papers

Civil service exams are usually identified by number only. You will be assigned a number; you must not put your name on your test papers. Be sure to copy your number correctly. Since more than one exam may be given, copy your exact examination title.

4) Plan your time

Unless you are told that a test is a "speed" or "rate of work" test, speed itself is usually not important. Time enough to answer all the questions will be provided, but this does not mean that you have all day. An overall time limit has been set. Divide the total time (in minutes) by the number of questions to determine the approximate time you have for each question.

5) Do not linger over difficult questions

If you come across a difficult question, mark it with a paper clip (useful to have along) and come back to it when you have been through the booklet. One caution if you do this – be sure to skip a number on your answer sheet as well. Check often to be sure that you have not lost your place and that you are marking in the row numbered the same as the question you are answering.

6) Read the questions

Be sure you know what the question asks! Many capable people are unsuccessful because they failed to *read* the questions correctly.

7) Answer all questions

Unless you have been instructed that a penalty will be deducted for incorrect answers, it is better to guess than to omit a question.

8) Speed tests

It is often better NOT to guess on speed tests. It has been found that on timed tests people are tempted to spend the last few seconds before time is called in marking answers at random – without even reading them – in the hope of picking up a few extra points. To discourage this practice, the instructions may warn you that your score will be "corrected" for guessing. That is, a penalty will be applied. The incorrect answers will be deducted from the correct ones, or some other penalty formula will be used.

9) Review your answers

If you finish before time is called, go back to the questions you guessed or omitted to give them further thought. Review other answers if you have time.

10) Return your test materials

If you are ready to leave before others have finished or time is called, take ALL your materials to the monitor and leave quietly. Never take any test material with you. The monitor can discover whose papers are not complete, and taking a test booklet may be grounds for disqualification.

VIII. EXAMINATION TECHNIQUES

1) Read the general instructions carefully. These are usually printed on the first page of the exam booklet. As a rule, these instructions refer to the timing of the examination; the fact that you should not start work until the signal and must stop work at a signal, etc. If there are any *special* instructions, such as a choice of questions to be answered, make sure that you note this instruction carefully.

2) When you are ready to start work on the examination, that is as soon as the signal has been given, read the instructions to each question booklet, underline any key words or phrases, such as *least, best, outline, describe* and the like. In this way you will tend to answer as requested rather than discover on reviewing your paper that you *listed without describing*, that you selected the *worst* choice rather than the *best* choice, etc.

3) If the examination is of the objective or multiple-choice type – that is, each question will also give a series of possible answers: A, B, C or D, and you are called upon to select the best answer and write the letter next to that answer on your answer paper – it is advisable to start answering each question in turn. There may be anywhere from 50 to 100 such questions in the three or four hours allotted and you can see how much time would be taken if you read through all the questions before beginning to answer any. Furthermore, if you come across a question or group of questions which you know would be difficult to answer, it would undoubtedly affect your handling of all the other questions.

4) If the examination is of the essay type and contains but a few questions, it is a moot point as to whether you should read all the questions before starting to answer any one. Of course, if you are given a choice – say five out of seven and the like – then it is essential to read all the questions so you can eliminate the two that are most difficult. If, however, you are asked to answer all the questions, there may be danger in trying to answer the easiest one first because you may find that you will spend too much time on it. The best technique is to answer the first question, then proceed to the second, etc.

5) Time your answers. Before the exam begins, write down the time it started, then add the time allowed for the examination and write down the time it must be completed, then divide the time available somewhat as follows:
    - If 3-1/2 hours are allowed, that would be 210 minutes. If you have 80 objective-type questions, that would be an average of 2-1/2 minutes per question. Allow yourself no more than 2 minutes per question, or a total of 160 minutes, which will permit about 50 minutes to review.
    - If for the time allotment of 210 minutes there are 7 essay questions to answer, that would average about 30 minutes a question. Give yourself only 25 minutes per question so that you have about 35 minutes to review.

6) The most important instruction is to *read each question* and make sure you know what is wanted. The second most important instruction is to *time yourself properly* so that you answer every question. The third most important instruction is to *answer every question*. Guess if you have to but include something for each question. Remember that you will receive no credit for a blank and will probably receive some credit if you write something in answer to an essay question. If you guess a letter – say "B" for a multiple-choice question – you may have guessed right. If you leave a blank as an answer to a multiple-choice question, the examiners may respect your feelings but it will not add a point to your score. Some exams may penalize you for wrong answers, so in such cases *only*, you may not want to guess unless you have some basis for your answer.

7) Suggestions
    a. Objective-type questions
        1. Examine the question booklet for proper sequence of pages and questions
        2. Read all instructions carefully
        3. Skip any question which seems too difficult; return to it after all other questions have been answered
        4. Apportion your time properly; do not spend too much time on any single question or group of questions

5. Note and underline key words – *all, most, fewest, least, best, worst, same, opposite*, etc.
6. Pay particular attention to negatives
7. Note unusual option, e.g., unduly long, short, complex, different or similar in content to the body of the question
8. Observe the use of "hedging" words – *probably, may, most likely*, etc.
9. Make sure that your answer is put next to the same number as the question
10. Do not second-guess unless you have good reason to believe the second answer is definitely more correct
11. Cross out original answer if you decide another answer is more accurate; do not erase until you are ready to hand your paper in
12. Answer all questions; guess unless instructed otherwise
13. Leave time for review

  b. Essay questions
    1. Read each question carefully
    2. Determine exactly what is wanted. Underline key words or phrases.
    3. Decide on outline or paragraph answer
    4. Include many different points and elements unless asked to develop any one or two points or elements
    5. Show impartiality by giving pros and cons unless directed to select one side only
    6. Make and write down any assumptions you find necessary to answer the questions
    7. Watch your English, grammar, punctuation and choice of words
    8. Time your answers; don't crowd material

8) Answering the essay question

Most essay questions can be answered by framing the specific response around several key words or ideas. Here are a few such key words or ideas:

M's: manpower, materials, methods, money, management
P's: purpose, program, policy, plan, procedure, practice, problems, pitfalls, personnel, public relations

  a. Six basic steps in handling problems:
    1. Preliminary plan and background development
    2. Collect information, data and facts
    3. Analyze and interpret information, data and facts
    4. Analyze and develop solutions as well as make recommendations
    5. Prepare report and sell recommendations
    6. Install recommendations and follow up effectiveness

  b. Pitfalls to avoid
    1. *Taking things for granted* – A statement of the situation does not necessarily imply that each of the elements is necessarily true; for example, a complaint may be invalid and biased so that all that can be taken for granted is that a complaint has been registered

2. *Considering only one side of a situation* – Wherever possible, indicate several alternatives and then point out the reasons you selected the best one
3. *Failing to indicate follow up* – Whenever your answer indicates action on your part, make certain that you will take proper follow-up action to see how successful your recommendations, procedures or actions turn out to be
4. *Taking too long in answering any single question* – Remember to time your answers properly

IX. AFTER THE TEST

Scoring procedures differ in detail among civil service jurisdictions although the general principles are the same. Whether the papers are hand-scored or graded by machine we have described, they are nearly always graded by number. That is, the person who marks the paper knows only the number – never the name – of the applicant. Not until all the papers have been graded will they be matched with names. If other tests, such as training and experience or oral interview ratings have been given, scores will be combined. Different parts of the examination usually have different weights. For example, the written test might count 60 percent of the final grade, and a rating of training and experience 40 percent. In many jurisdictions, veterans will have a certain number of points added to their grades.

After the final grade has been determined, the names are placed in grade order and an eligible list is established. There are various methods for resolving ties between those who get the same final grade – probably the most common is to place first the name of the person whose application was received first. Job offers are made from the eligible list in the order the names appear on it. You will be notified of your grade and your rank as soon as all these computations have been made. This will be done as rapidly as possible.

People who are found to meet the requirements in the announcement are called "eligibles." Their names are put on a list of eligible candidates. An eligible's chances of getting a job depend on how high he stands on this list and how fast agencies are filling jobs from the list.

When a job is to be filled from a list of eligibles, the agency asks for the names of people on the list of eligibles for that job. When the civil service commission receives this request, it sends to the agency the names of the three people highest on this list. Or, if the job to be filled has specialized requirements, the office sends the agency the names of the top three persons who meet these requirements from the general list.

The appointing officer makes a choice from among the three people whose names were sent to him. If the selected person accepts the appointment, the names of the others are put back on the list to be considered for future openings.

That is the rule in hiring from all kinds of eligible lists, whether they are for typist, carpenter, chemist, or something else. For every vacancy, the appointing officer has his choice of any one of the top three eligibles on the list. This explains why the person whose name is on top of the list sometimes does not get an appointment when some of the persons lower on the list do. If the appointing officer chooses the second or third eligible, the No. 1 eligible does not get a job at once, but stays on the list until he is appointed or the list is terminated.

X. HOW TO PASS THE INTERVIEW TEST

The examination for which you applied requires an oral interview test. You have already taken the written test and you are now being called for the interview test – the final part of the formal examination.

You may think that it is not possible to prepare for an interview test and that there are no procedures to follow during an interview. Our purpose is to point out some things you can do in advance that will help you and some good rules to follow and pitfalls to avoid while you are being interviewed.

What is an interview supposed to test?

The written examination is designed to test the technical knowledge and competence of the candidate; the oral is designed to evaluate intangible qualities, not readily measured otherwise, and to establish a list showing the relative fitness of each candidate – as measured against his competitors – for the position sought. Scoring is not on the basis of "right" and "wrong," but on a sliding scale of values ranging from "not passable" to "outstanding." As a matter of fact, it is possible to achieve a relatively low score without a single "incorrect" answer because of evident weakness in the qualities being measured.

Occasionally, an examination may consist entirely of an oral test – either an individual or a group oral. In such cases, information is sought concerning the technical knowledges and abilities of the candidate, since there has been no written examination for this purpose. More commonly, however, an oral test is used to supplement a written examination.

Who conducts interviews?

The composition of oral boards varies among different jurisdictions. In nearly all, a representative of the personnel department serves as chairman. One of the members of the board may be a representative of the department in which the candidate would work. In some cases, "outside experts" are used, and, frequently, a businessman or some other representative of the general public is asked to serve. Labor and management or other special groups may be represented. The aim is to secure the services of experts in the appropriate field.

However the board is composed, it is a good idea (and not at all improper or unethical) to ascertain in advance of the interview who the members are and what groups they represent. When you are introduced to them, you will have some idea of their backgrounds and interests, and at least you will not stutter and stammer over their names.

What should be done before the interview?

While knowledge about the board members is useful and takes some of the surprise element out of the interview, there is other preparation which is more substantive. It *is* possible to prepare for an oral interview – in several ways:

1) Keep a copy of your application and review it carefully before the interview

This may be the only document before the oral board, and the starting point of the interview. Know what education and experience you have listed there, and the sequence and dates of all of it. Sometimes the board will ask you to review the highlights of your experience for them; you should not have to hem and haw doing it.

2) Study the class specification and the examination announcement

Usually, the oral board has one or both of these to guide them. The qualities, characteristics or knowledges required by the position sought are stated in these documents. They offer valuable clues as to the nature of the oral interview. For example, if the job involves supervisory responsibilities, the announcement will usually indicate that knowledge of modern supervisory methods and the qualifications of the candidate as a supervisor will be tested. If so, you can expect such questions, frequently in the form of a hypothetical situation which you are expected to solve. NEVER go into an oral without knowledge of the duties and responsibilities of the job you seek.

3) Think through each qualification required

Try to visualize the kind of questions you would ask if you were a board member. How well could you answer them? Try especially to appraise your own knowledge and background in each area, *measured against the job sought*, and identify any areas in which you are weak. Be critical and realistic – do not flatter yourself.

4) Do some general reading in areas in which you feel you may be weak

For example, if the job involves supervision and your past experience has NOT, some general reading in supervisory methods and practices, particularly in the field of human relations, might be useful. Do NOT study agency procedures or detailed manuals. The oral board will be testing your understanding and capacity, not your memory.

5) Get a good night's sleep and watch your general health and mental attitude

You will want a clear head at the interview. Take care of a cold or any other minor ailment, and of course, no hangovers.

What should be done on the day of the interview?

Now comes the day of the interview itself. Give yourself plenty of time to get there. Plan to arrive somewhat ahead of the scheduled time, particularly if your appointment is in the fore part of the day. If a previous candidate fails to appear, the board might be ready for you a bit early. By early afternoon an oral board is almost invariably behind schedule if there are many candidates, and you may have to wait. Take along a book or magazine to read, or your application to review, but leave any extraneous material in the waiting room when you go in for your interview. In any event, relax and compose yourself.

The matter of dress is important. The board is forming impressions about you – from your experience, your manners, your attitude, and your appearance. Give your personal appearance careful attention. Dress your best, but not your flashiest. Choose conservative, appropriate clothing, and be sure it is immaculate. This is a business interview, and your appearance should indicate that you regard it as such. Besides, being well groomed and properly dressed will help boost your confidence.

Sooner or later, someone will call your name and escort you into the interview room. *This is it.* From here on you are on your own. It is too late for any more preparation. But remember, you asked for this opportunity to prove your fitness, and you are here because your request was granted.

What happens when you go in?

The usual sequence of events will be as follows: The clerk (who is often the board stenographer) will introduce you to the chairman of the oral board, who will introduce you to the other members of the board. Acknowledge the introductions before you sit down. Do not be surprised if you find a microphone facing you or a stenotypist sitting by. Oral interviews are usually recorded in the event of an appeal or other review.

Usually the chairman of the board will open the interview by reviewing the highlights of your education and work experience from your application – primarily for the benefit of the other members of the board, as well as to get the material into the record. Do not interrupt or comment unless there is an error or significant misinterpretation; if that is the case, do not hesitate. But do not quibble about insignificant matters. Also, he will usually ask you some question about your education, experience or your present job – partly to get you to start talking and to establish the interviewing "rapport." He may start the actual questioning, or turn it over to one of the other members. Frequently, each member undertakes the questioning on a particular area, one in which he is perhaps most competent, so you can expect each member to participate in the examination. Because time is limited, you may also expect some rather abrupt switches in the direction the questioning takes, so do not be upset by it. Normally, a board member will not pursue a single line of questioning unless he discovers a particular strength or weakness.

After each member has participated, the chairman will usually ask whether any member has any further questions, then will ask you if you have anything you wish to add. Unless you are expecting this question, it may floor you. Worse, it may start you off on an extended, extemporaneous speech. The board is not usually seeking more information. The question is principally to offer you a last opportunity to present further qualifications or to indicate that you have nothing to add. So, if you feel that a significant qualification or characteristic has been overlooked, it is proper to point it out in a sentence or so. Do not compliment the board on the thoroughness of their examination – they have been sketchy, and you know it. If you wish, merely say, "No thank you, I have nothing further to add." This is a point where you can "talk yourself out" of a good impression or fail to present an important bit of information. Remember, *you close the interview yourself.*

The chairman will then say, "That is all, Mr. _____, thank you." Do not be startled; the interview is over, and quicker than you think. Thank him, gather your belongings and take your leave. Save your sigh of relief for the other side of the door.

How to put your best foot forward

Throughout this entire process, you may feel that the board individually and collectively is trying to pierce your defenses, seek out your hidden weaknesses and embarrass and confuse you. Actually, this is not true. They are obliged to make an appraisal of your qualifications for the job you are seeking, and they want to see you in your best light. Remember, they must interview all candidates and a non-cooperative candidate may become a failure in spite of their best efforts to bring out his qualifications. Here are 15 suggestions that will help you:

1) Be natural – Keep your attitude confident, not cocky

If you are not confident that you can do the job, do not expect the board to be. Do not apologize for your weaknesses, try to bring out your strong points. The board is interested in a positive, not negative, presentation. Cockiness will antagonize any board member and make him wonder if you are covering up a weakness by a false show of strength.

2) Get comfortable, but don't lounge or sprawl

Sit erectly but not stiffly. A careless posture may lead the board to conclude that you are careless in other things, or at least that you are not impressed by the importance of the occasion. Either conclusion is natural, even if incorrect. Do not fuss with your clothing, a pencil or an ashtray. Your hands may occasionally be useful to emphasize a point; do not let them become a point of distraction.

3) Do not wisecrack or make small talk

This is a serious situation, and your attitude should show that you consider it as such. Further, the time of the board is limited – they do not want to waste it, and neither should you.

4) Do not exaggerate your experience or abilities

In the first place, from information in the application or other interviews and sources, the board may know more about you than you think. Secondly, you probably will not get away with it. An experienced board is rather adept at spotting such a situation, so do not take the chance.

5) If you know a board member, do not make a point of it, yet do not hide it

Certainly you are not fooling him, and probably not the other members of the board. Do not try to take advantage of your acquaintanceship – it will probably do you little good.

6) Do not dominate the interview

Let the board do that. They will give you the clues – do not assume that you have to do all the talking. Realize that the board has a number of questions to ask you, and do not try to take up all the interview time by showing off your extensive knowledge of the answer to the first one.

7) Be attentive

You only have 20 minutes or so, and you should keep your attention at its sharpest throughout. When a member is addressing a problem or question to you, give him your undivided attention. Address your reply principally to him, but do not exclude the other board members.

8) Do not interrupt

A board member may be stating a problem for you to analyze. He will ask you a question when the time comes. Let him state the problem, and wait for the question.

9) Make sure you understand the question

Do not try to answer until you are sure what the question is. If it is not clear, restate it in your own words or ask the board member to clarify it for you. However, do not haggle about minor elements.

10) Reply promptly but not hastily

A common entry on oral board rating sheets is "candidate responded readily," or "candidate hesitated in replies." Respond as promptly and quickly as you can, but do not jump to a hasty, ill-considered answer.

11) Do not be peremptory in your answers

A brief answer is proper – but do not fire your answer back. That is a losing game from your point of view. The board member can probably ask questions much faster than you can answer them.

12) Do not try to create the answer you think the board member wants

He is interested in what kind of mind you have and how it works – not in playing games. Furthermore, he can usually spot this practice and will actually grade you down on it.

13) Do not switch sides in your reply merely to agree with a board member

Frequently, a member will take a contrary position merely to draw you out and to see if you are willing and able to defend your point of view. Do not start a debate, yet do not surrender a good position. If a position is worth taking, it is worth defending.

14) Do not be afraid to admit an error in judgment if you are shown to be wrong

The board knows that you are forced to reply without any opportunity for careful consideration. Your answer may be demonstrably wrong. If so, admit it and get on with the interview.

15) Do not dwell at length on your present job

The opening question may relate to your present assignment. Answer the question but do not go into an extended discussion. You are being examined for a *new* job, not your present one. As a matter of fact, try to phrase ALL your answers in terms of the job for which you are being examined.

Basis of Rating

Probably you will forget most of these "do's" and "don'ts" when you walk into the oral interview room. Even remembering them all will not ensure you a passing grade. Perhaps you did not have the qualifications in the first place. But remembering them will help you to put your best foot forward, without treading on the toes of the board members.

Rumor and popular opinion to the contrary notwithstanding, an oral board wants you to make the best appearance possible. They know you are under pressure – but they also want to see how you respond to it as a guide to what your reaction would be under the pressures of the job you seek. They will be influenced by the degree of poise you display, the personal traits you show and the manner in which you respond.

ABOUT THIS BOOK

This book contains tests divided into Examination Sections. Go through each test, answering every question in the margin. We have also attached a sample answer sheet at the back of the book that can be removed and used. At the end of each test look at the answer key and check your answers. On the ones you got wrong, look at the right answer choice and learn. Do not fill in the answers first. Do not memorize the questions and answers, but understand the answer and principles involved. On your test, the questions will likely be different from the samples. Questions are changed and new ones added. If you understand these past questions you should have success with any changes that arise. Tests may consist of several types of questions. We have additional books on each subject should more study be advisable or necessary for you. Finally, the more you study, the better prepared you will be. This book is intended to be the last thing you study before you walk into the examination room. Prior study of relevant texts is also recommended. NLC publishes some of these in our Fundamental Series. Knowledge and good sense are important factors in passing your exam. Good luck also helps. So now study this Passbook, absorb the material contained within and take that knowledge into the examination. Then do your best to pass that exam.

EXAMINATION SECTION

EXAMINATION SECTION
TEST 1

DIRECTIONS: Each question or incomplete statement is followed by several suggested answers or completions. Select the one that *BEST* answers the question or completes the statement. *PRINT THE LETTER OF THE CORRECT ANSWER IN THE SPACE AT THE RIGHT.*

1. The MOST important characteristic of a tickler card file is that the cards are arranged according to

   A. subject matter
   B. the date on which action is to be taken
   C. the name of the individual on the card
   D. the order of importance of the items contained on the cards

   1._____

2. As a clerk in a city department, one of your duties is to maintain the files in your bureau. Material from these files is sometimes used by other bureaus. You frequently find that you are unable to locate some material because it has been removed from the files and is evidently being used by some other bureau. The BEST way to correct this situation is to

   A. have an out-of-file card filled out and filed when ever material is borrowed from the files
   B. forbid employees of other bureaus to borrow material from the files unless they promise to return it promptly
   C. provide other bureaus with duplicate files
   D. notify your supervisor whenever an employee from another bureau is slow in returning material to the files

   2._____

3. A transfer file is used primarily to

   A. carry records from one office to another
   B. store inactive records
   C. hold records that are constantly used by more than one bureau of an organization
   D. hold confidential records

   3._____

4. When a record is borrowed from the files, the file clerk puts a substitution or *out* card in its place. Of the following, the information that is LEAST commonly placed on the *out* card is

   A. who borrowed the record
   B. when the record was borrowed
   C. why the record was borrowed
   D. what record was borrowed

   4._____

5. It is frequently helpful to file material under two subjects. In such a case the material is filed under one subject and a card indicating where the material is filed is placed under the other subject. This card is known generally as a

   A. follow-up or tickler card   B. guide card
   C. transfer card   D. cross-reference card

   5._____

1

6. Of the following, for which reason are cross-references necessary in filing?

   A. there is a choice of terms under which the correspondence may be filed
   B. the only filing information contained in the correspondence is the name of the writer
   C. records are immediately visible without searching through the files
   D. persons other than file clerks can easily locate material

7. In filing, a clerk must often attach several papers together before placing them in the files. Usually, the MOST desirable of the following methods of attaching these papers is to

   A. pin them together
   B. staple them together
   C. attach them with a paper clip
   D. glue them together

8. A clerk employed in the central file section of a city department has been requested to obtain a certain card which is kept in an alphabetic file containing several thousand cards, The clerk finds that this card is not in its proper place and that there is no *out* card to aid him in tracing its location. Of the following, the course of action which would be LEAST helpful to him in locating the missing card would be for him to

   A. secure the assistance of his superior
   B. look at several cards filed immediately before and after the place where the missing card should be filed
   C. ask the other clerks in the file section whether they have this card
   D. prepare an *out* card and place it where the missing card should be filed

9. A clerk assigned to file correspondence in a subject file would be MOST concerned with the

   A. name of the sender
   B. main topic of the correspondence
   C. city and state of the sender
   D. date of the correspondence

10. Filing, in a way, is a form of recording. The one of the following which BEST explains this statement is that

    A. no other records are required if a proper filing system is used
    B. important records should, as a rule, be kept in filing cabinets
    C. a good system of record keeping eliminates the necessity for a filing system
    D. filing a letter or document is, in effect, equivalent to making a record of its contents

11. Of the following, a centralized filing system is LEAST suitable for filing

    A. material which is confidential in nature
    B. routine correspondence
    C. periodic reports of the divisions of the department
    D. material used by several divisions of the department

12. *A misplaced record is a lost record.* Of the following, the most valid implication of this statement in regard to office work is that

    A. all records in an office should be filed in strict alphabetical order
    B. accuracy in filing is essential
    C. only one method of filing should be used throughout the office
    D. files should be locked when not in use

13. Suppose that you are in charge of a unit which maintains a rather intricate filing system. A new file clerk has been added to your staff. Of the following assignments that may be given to this clerk, the one which requires the LEAST amount of knowledge of the filing system is

    A. placing material in the files
    B. removing papers from the files
    C. classifying and coding material for filing
    D. keeping a record of material taken from, and returned to, the files

14. Which one of the following is the MOST important objective of filing?

    A. Giving a secretary something to do in her spare time
    B. Making it possible to locate information quickly
    C. Providing a place to store unneeded documents
    D. Keeping extra papers from accumulating on workers' desks

15. Which one of the following BEST describes the usual arrangement of a tickler file?

    A. Alphabetical
    B. Chronological
    C. Numerical
    D. Geographical

16. Which one of the following is the LEAST desirable filing practice?

    A. Using staples to keep papers together
    B. Filing all material without regard to date
    C. Keeping a record of all materials removed from the files
    D. Writing filing instructions on each paper prior to filing

17. The *one* of the following records which it would be MOST advisable to keep in *alphabetical order* is a

    A. continuous listing of phone messages, including time and caller, for your supervisor
    B. listing of individuals currently employed by your agency in a particular title
    C. record of purchases paid for by the petty cash fund
    D. dated record of employees who have borrowed material from the files in your office

18. Assume that, in an office of a city agency, correspondence is filed, according to the date received, in 12 folders, one for each month of the year. On January 1 of each year, correspondence dated through December 31 of the preceding year is transferred from the active to the inactive files. New folders are then inserted in the active files to contain the correspondence to be filed in the next year. The one of the following which is the chief disadvantage of this method of transferring correspondence from active to inactive files is that

A. the inactive files may lack the capacity to contain all the correspondence transferred to them
B. the folders prepared each year must be labeled the same as the folders in preceding years
C. some of the correspondence from the preceding year may not be in the active files on January 1
D. some of the correspondence transferred to the inactive files may be referred to as frequently as some of the correspondence in the active files

19. The central filing unit of a certain city department keeps in its files records used by the various bureaus in connection with their daily work. It is desirable for the clerks in this filing unit to refile records as soon as possible after they have been returned by the different bureaus CHIEFLY because

    A. records which are needed can be located most easily if they have been filed
    B. such procedure develops commendable work habits among the employees
    C. records which are not filed immediately are ususally filed incorrectly
    D. the accumulation of records to be filed gives the office a disorderly appearance

20. The active and inactive file material of an office is to be filed in several four-drawer filing cabinets. Of the following, the BEST method of filing the material is, in general, to

    A. keep inactive material in the upper drawers of the file cabinet so that such material may be easily removed for disposal
    B. keep active material in the upper drawers so that the amount of stooping by clerks using the files is reduced to a minimum
    C. assign drawers in the file cabinets alternately to active and to inactive material so that file material can be transferred easily from the active to the inactive files
    D. assign file cabinets alternately to active and to inactive material so that cross-references between the two types of material can be easily made

---

KEY (CORRECT ANSWERS)

1.	B	11.	A
2.	A	12.	B
3.	B	13.	D
4.	C	14.	B
5.	D	15.	B
6.	A	16.	B
7.	B	17.	B
8.	D	18.	D
9.	B	19.	A
10.	D	20.	B

TEST 2

DIRECTIONS: Each question or incomplete statement is followed by several suggested answers or completions. Select the one that BEST answers the question or completes the statement. PRINT THE LETTER OF THE CORRECT ANSWER IN THE SPACE AT THE RIGHT.

1. Suppose you are checking an alphabetical card reference file to locate information about a *George Dyerly*. After checking all the *D's* you can find a card only for a *George Dyrely*. Of the following, the BEST action for you to take is to

    A. check the balance of the file to see if the card you are interested in has been misfiled
    B. check the data on the card to see if it relates to the same person in whom you are interested
    C. correct the spelling of the name on your records and reports to conform to the spelling on the card
    D. reject this reference file as a source of information regarding this person

    1.____

2. Assume that you have been assigned by your supervisor to file some record cards in a cabinet. All the cards in this cabinet are supposed to be kept in strict alphabetical order. You know that important work is being held up because certain cards in this cabinet cannot be located. While filing the records given you, you come across a card which is not in its correct alphabetical place. Of the following, the BEST reason for you to bring this record to the attention of your supervisor is that

    A. errors in filing are more serious than other types of errors
    B. your alertness in locating the card should be rewarded
    C. the filing system may be at fault, rather than the employee who misfiled the card
    D. time may be saved by such action

    2.____

3. A *tickler file* is used CHIEFLY for

    A. unsorted papers which the file clerk has not had time to file
    B. personnel records
    C. pending matters which should receive attention at some particular time
    D. index to cross-referenced material

    3.____

4. A new file clerk who has not become thoroughly familiar with the files is unable to locate *McLeod* in the correspondence files under *Mc* and asks your help. Of the following, the BEST reply to give her is that

    A. there probably is no correspondence in the files for that person
    B. she probably has the name spelled wrong and should verify the spelling
    C. she will probably find the correspondence under *McLeod* as the files are arranged with the prefix *Mc* considered as *Mac* (as if the name were spelled *MacLeod*).
    D. the correspondence folder for *McLeod* has evidently been misplaced or borrowed from the files

    4.____

5. Assume you are in an office which uses a subject filing system. You find that frequently a letter to be filed involves two or three subjects. In filing such a letter, it is MOST important to

    A. file it under the subject that is mentioned first in the letter
    B. prepare cross-references for the subjects covered in the letter

    5.____

C. list all subjects involved on the label of the file folder
D. code the letter to show the main subject and its subdivisions

6. The MOST frequently used filing system in ordinary office practice is the

    A. alphabetic system   B. numeric system
    C. geographic system   D. subject system

7. If you wanted to check on the accuracy of the filing in your unit, you would

    A. check all the files thoroughly at regular intervals
    B. watch the clerks while they are filing
    C. glance through filed papers at random
    D. inspect thoroughly a small section of the files selected at random

8. The decision of a secretary to set up and maintain a subject filing system is MOST justified if

    A. speed in placing material in the files is of primary importance
    B. she is generally asked to obtain all the filed material dealing with a particular transaction or topic
    C. the system must be simple enough to permit its use by practically any employee with a little knowledge of filing
    D. there is to be no need to classify material before filing it

9. Several filing operaitons are performed by a secretary in operating and maintaining a subject filing system. Of the filing operations, the two which the secretary can MOST practicably perform at the same time are

    A. coding and placing material in the files
    B. classifying and placing material in the files
    C. placing material in the files and charging out borrowed material
    D. classifying and coding material for the files

10. Of the following systems of filing, the one that is considered the best for safeguarding confidential records is the

    A. alphabetical   B. numerical
    C. geographical   D. subject

11. While working in a clinic, you discover some obvious inconsistencies in the filing system as a whole. You also have in mind a corrective measure which you would like to see put into practice. The one of the following which is the MOST acceptable procedure for you to follow is to

    A. try out your new system for a few days to determine its success before discussing it with your supervisor
    B. explain the probable advantages of your proposed plan to your supervisor and secure his approval before making any changes
    C. continue working under the old procedure until the inconsistencies become apparent to the rest of the staff
    D. collect sufficient evidence to prove the obvious inconsistencies in the present filing system in order to convince your supervisor that the system is unsatisfactory

12. Assume that you are in charge of the patients' files in the health center to which you are assigned. The record cards of the individual patients are filed alphabetically according to the name of the patient. You want to make it easier to pick out the cards of those patients who are under treatment for any one of five indicated diseases. Of the following, the procedure which would be MOST helpful for this purpose would be to

    A. insert the card of each patient having one of the five diseases into a special folder
    B. use a different size card for each of the five diseases
    C. use a different color card for each of the five diseases
    D. underline the name of the disease on each card in the file

13. When papers are filed according to the date of their receipt, they are said to be filed

    A. numerically
    B. geographically
    C. chronologically
    D. alphabetically

14. The one of the following which is the MOST important requirement of a good filing system is that

    A. the expense of installation and operation be low
    B. papers be found easily when needed
    C. the system be capable of any amount of expansion which may be necessary in the future
    D. the filing system have a cross-reference index

15. The MAIN purpose of transferring materials from active to inactive files is to

    A. keep current reference files from growing to a size where they become inefficient and unmanageable
    B. distinguish between important business and less important matters
    C. provide a means of storing letters that need not be answered
    D. make sure that there is some way of retrieving information from previous years

16. The one of the following for which a cross-index is *most likely* to be needed is a

    A. file of reference material arranged by subject
    B. file of individual personnel records arranged alphabetically
    C. card file containing addresses and phone numbers for various organizations
    D. supervisor's *tickler file*

17. The CHIEF advantage of a rotary file is that

    A. it holds much more material than a standard file cabinet
    B. it provides a temporary location for material that is due to be placed in the permanent files
    C. items can be easily located and scanned without being removed from the file
    D. less time is required for placing an item on a rotary file than for placing it in a standard upright file

18. In a miscellaneous correspondence folder in a file drawer, it is *usually* MOST helpful if letters are arranged according to

    A. date with the most recent date on the bottom
    B. date with the most recent date on the top

C. subject with the subjects alphabetically arranged
D. name with the names arranged geographically

19. Assume that you are responsible for maintaining the patients' medical record file in the clinic to which you are assigned. Frequently, the other clinics in the health center where you work borrow record cards from your clinic files.
The BEST way for you to avoid difficulty in locating cards which may have been borrowed by other clinics is to

   A. make out a duplicate card for any clinic that wishes to borrow a card from your file
   B. refuse to lend your card to any other clinic unless the other clinic's personnel officer promises to return the card in person
   C. report it to your supervisor if anyone fails to return a card after a reasonable time
   D. have the person who borrows a card fill out an out-of-file card and place it in the file whenever a record card is removed

20. Suppose that you are given an unalphabetized list of 500 clinic patients and a set of unalphabetized record cards. Your supervisor asks you to determine if there is a record card for each patient whose name is on the list. For you to first arrange the medical record cards in alphabetical order BEFORE checking them with the names on the list is

   A. *desirable;* this will make it easier to check each name on the list against the patients' record cards
   B. *undesirable;* it is just as easy to alphabetize the names on the list as it is to rearrange the record cards
   C. *desirable;* this extra work with the record cards will give you more information about the patients
   D. *undesirable;* adding an extra step to the procedure makes the work too complicated

KEY (CORRECT ANSWERS)

1. B
2. D
3. C
4. C
5. B

6. A
7. D
8. B
9. D
10. B

11. B
12. C
13. C
14. B
15. A

16. A
17. C
18. B
19. D
20. A

TEST 3

DIRECTIONS: Each question or incomplete statement is followed by several suggested answers or completions. Select the one that *BEST* answers the question or completes the statement. *PRINT THE LETTER OF THE CORRECT ANSWER IN THE SPACE AT THE RIGHT.*

1. Of the following, for which reason are cross-references necessary in filing?　　　　1.____

    A. There is a choice of terms under which the correspondence may be filed.
    B. The only filing information contained in the correspondence is the name of the writer.
    C. Records are immediately visible without searching through the files.
    D. Persons other than file clerks can easily locate material.

2. Suppose that the name files in your office contain filing guides on which appear the letters of the alphabet. The letters X, Y, and Z, unlike the other letters of the alphabet, are grouped together and appear on a single guide. Of the following, the BEST reason for combining these three letters into a single filing unit is probably that　　　　2.____

    A. provision must be made for expanding the file if that should become necessary
    B. there is usually insufficient room for filing guides towards the end of a long file
    C. the letters X, Y, and Z are at the end of the alphabet
    D. relatively few names begin with these letters of the alphabet

3. You are requested by your supervisor to replace each card you take out of the files with an *out-of-file* slip. The *out-of-file* slip indicates which card has been removed from the file and where the card may be found. Of the following the CHIEF value of the *out-of-file* slip is that a clerk looking for a card which happens to have been removed by another clerk　　　　3.____

    A. will know that the card has been returned to the file
    B. can substitute the *out-of-file* slip for the original card
    C. will not waste time searching for the card under the impression that it has been misfiled
    D. is not likely to misfile a card he has been using for some other purpose

4. Suppose that is is the practice, in your department, to file all the correspondence with one individual in a single folder and to file the most recent letters first in the folder. Of the following, the BEST justification for placing the most recent letter first rather than last in the folder is that, in general,　　　　4.____

    A. letters placed in front of a folder are usually less accessible
    B. requests for previous correspondence from the files usually concern letters filed relatively recently
    C. letters in a folder can usually be lcoated most quickly when they are filed in a definite order
    D. filing can usually be accomplished very quickly when letters are placed in a folder without reference to date

5. While filing cards in an alphabetical file, you notice a card which is not in its correct alphabetical order. Of the following the BEST action for you take is to　　　　5.____

    A. show the card to your supervisor and ask him whether that card has been reported lost

9

B. leave the card where it is, but inform the other clerks who use the file exactly where they may find the card if they need it
C. file a cross-reference card in the place where the card should have been filed
D. make a written notation of where you can find the card in the event that your supervisor asks you for it

6. A new alphabetical name card file covering fifteen file drawers has been set up in your office. Your supervisor asks you to place identifying labels outside each file drawer. Of the following, the BEST rule for you to follow in determining the appropriate label for each drawer is that

   A. the alphabet should be divided equally among the file drawers available
   B. each label should give the beginning and ending points of the cards in that drawer
   C. each drawer should begin with a new letter of the alphabet
   D. no drawer should contain more than two letters of the alphabet

7. One of the administrators in your department cannot find an important letter left on his desk. He believes that the letter may accidentally have been placed among a group of letters sent to you for filing. You look in the file and find the letter filed in its correct place. Of the following, the BEST suggestion for you to make to your supervisor in order to avoid repetition of such incidents is that

   A. file clerks should be permitted to read material they are requested to.
   B. correspondence files should be cross-indexed
   C. a periodic check should be made of the files to locate material inaccurately filed
   D. material which is sent to the file clerk should be marked *OK for filing.*

8. One of your duties is to keep a file of administrative orders by date. Your supervisor often asks you to find the order concerning a particular subject. Since you are rarely able to remember the date of the order, it is necessary for you to search through the entire file. Of the following, the BEST suggestion for you to make to your supervisor for remedying this situation is that

   A. each order bear conspicuously in its upper left hand corner the precise date on which it is issued
   B. old orders be taken from the file and destroyed as soon as they are superseded by new orders, so that the file will not be overcrowded
   C. an alphabetic subject index of orders be prepared so that orders can be located easily by content as well as date
   D. dates be eliminated entirely from orders

9. It is important that every office have a retention and disposal program for filing material. Suppose that you have been appointed administrative assistant in an office with a poorly organized records retention program. In establishing a revised program for the transfer or disposal of records, the step which would logically be taken THIRD in the process is

   A. preparing a safe and inexpensive storage area and setting up an indexing system for records already in storage
   B. determining what papers to retain and for how long a period
   C. taking an inventory of what is filed, where it is filed, how much is filed and how often it is used
   D. moving records from active to inactive files and destroying useless records

10. In evaluating the effectiveness of a filing system, the one of the following criteria which you should consider MOST important is the

   A. safety of material in the event of a fire
   B. ease with which material may be located
   C. quantity of papers which can be filed
   D. extent to which material in the filing system is being used

10.____

11. In a certain file room it is customary, when removing a record from the files, to insert an out card in its place. A clerk suggests keeping, in addition, a chronological list of all records removed and the names of the employees who have removed them. This suggestion would be of GREATEST value

   A. in avoiding duplication of work
   B. in enabling an employee to refile records
   C. where records are frequently misfiled
   D. where records are frequently kept out longer than necessary

11.____

12. You are given a large batch of correspondence and asked to obtain the folder on file for each of the senders of these letters. The folders in your file room are kept in numerical order and an alphabetic cross-index file is maintained. Of the following, the BEST procedure would be for you to

   A. look up the numbers in the alphabetic file, then alphabetize the correspondence according to the senders' names and obtain the folders from the numerical file
   B. alphabetize the correspondence according to the senders' names, get the file numbers from the alphabetic file and obtain the folders from the numerical file
   C. alphabetize the correspondence and then look through the numerical file for the proper folders in the order in which your correspondence is arranged
   D. look through the numerical file, pulling out the folders as you come across them

12.____

13. In filing terminology, coding means

   A. making a preliminary arrangement of names according to caption before bringing them together in final order of arrangement
   B. reading correspondence and determining the proper caption under which it is to be filed
   C. marking a card or paper with symbols or other means of identification to indicate where it is to be placed in the files according to a predetermined plan
   D. placing a card or paper in the files showing where correspondence may be located under another name or title

13.____

14. A duplex-number system of filing is a(n)

   A. decimal system
   B. arrangement of guides and folders with a definite color scheme to aid in filing and locating material
   C. system of filing by which classified subjects are divided and subdivided by number for the purpose of expansion
   D. method of filing names according to sound instead of spelling

14.____

15. A set of cards numbered from 1 to 300 has been filed in numerical order in such a way that the highest number is at the front of the file and lowest number is at the rear. It is desired that the cards be reversed to run in ascending order. The BEST of the following methods that can be used in performing this task is to

    A. begin at the front of the file and remove the cards one at a time, placing each one face up on top of the one removed before
    B. begin at the front of the file and remove the cards one at a time, placing each one face down on top of the one removed before
    C. begin at the back of the file and remove the cards in small groups, placing each group face down on top of the group removed before
    D. begin at the back of the file and remove the cards one at a time, placing each one face up on top of the one removed before

16. Confusion regarding the exact location of certain papers missing from files can probably BEST be avoided by

    A. using colored tabs
    B. using the Dewey Decimal System
    C. making files available to few persons
    D. consistently using *out* guides

17. The FIRST step in filing cards alphabetically is to

    A. count the cards
    B. divide the cards into groups of ten
    C. inspect each card to insure that it is filled out completely
    D. rearrange the cards in alphabetical order

18. If you cannot find the folder on Michael Hillston in an alphabetic file, you should

    A. assume that the folder is lost
    B. check other places where the folder could easily have been misfiled, like Hilston and Hillson
    C. look through all of the alphabetic files to see whether the folder was misplaced
    D. return to your other work and check for the folder again the next day

19. Of the following, the type of filing system used in the MOST efficiently run office depends *MOSTLY* on the

    A. way records are used or requested
    B. geographical location of the office
    C. skill of clerical personnel who do the filing
    D. number of filing clerks employed

20. The MOST important reason for well-organized files is to insure that

    A. business papers and records can easily be found
    B. company documents will be arranged alphabetically
    C. file space will be efficiently utilized for business purposes
    D. it is possible to identify the individual who committed any errors

KEY (CORRECT ANSWERS)

1. A
2. D
3. C
4. B
5. A

6. B
7. D
8. C
9. A
10. B

11. D
12. B
13. C
14. C
15. A

16. D
17. D
18. B
19. A
20. A

EXAMINATION SECTION

TEST 1

DIRECTIONS: Each question or incomplete statement is followed by several suggested answers or completions. Select the one that BEST answers the question or completes the statement. *PRINT THE LETTER OF THE CORRECT ANSWER IN THE SPACE AT THE RIGHT.*

1. A multi-line telephone with buttons for eight separate lines, plus a *hold* button, is often used when an office requires more than one outside line.
   If you are talking on one line of this type of office phone when another call comes in, what is the procedure to follow if you want to answer the second call but keep the first call on the line?
   Push the
   A. *hold* button at the same time as you push the *pickup* button of the ringing line
   B. *hold* button and then push the *pickup* button of the ringing line
   C. *pickup* button of the ringing line and then push the *hold* button
   D. *pickup* button of the ringing line and push the *hold* button when you return to the original line

   1.____

2. Suppose that you are asked to prepare a petty cash statement for March. The original and one copy are to go to the personnel office. One copy is to go to the fiscal office, and another copy is to go to your supervisor. The last copy is for your files.
   In preparing the statement and the copies, how many sheets of copy paper should you use?
   A. 3 B. 4 C. 5 D. 8

   2.____

3. Which one of the following is the LEAST important advantage of putting the subject of a letter in the heading to the right of the address? It
   A. makes filing of the copy easier
   B. makes more space available in the body of the letter
   C. simplifies distribution of letters
   D. simplifies determination of the subject of the letter

   3.____

4. Of the following, the MOST efficient way to put 100 copies of a one-page letter into 9½" x 4⅛" envelopes for mailing is to fold _____ into an envelope.
   A. each letter and insert it immediately after folding
   B. each letter separately until all 100 are folded; then insert each one
   C. the 100 letters two at a time, then separate them and insert each one
   D. two letters together, slip them apart, and insert each one

   4.____

5. When preparing papers for filing, it is NOT desirable to
   A. smooth papers that are wrinkled
   B. use paper clips to keep related papers together in the files
   C. arrange the papers in the order in which they will be filed
   D. mend torn papers with cellophane tape

6. Of the following, the BEST reason for a clerical unit to have its own duplicating machine is that the unit
   A. uses many forms which it must reproduce internally
   B. must make two copies of each piece of incoming mail for a special file
   C. must make seven copies of each piece of outgoing mail
   D. must type 200 envelopes each month for distribution to the same offices

7. Several offices use the same photocopying machine.
   If each office must pay its share of the cost of running this machine, the BEST way of determining how much of this cost should be charged to each of these offices is to
   A. determine the monthly number of photocopies made by each office
   B. determine the monthly number of originals submitted for photocopying by each office
   C. determine the number of times per day each office uses the photocopying machine
   D. divide the total cost of running the photocopy machine by the total number of offices using the machine

8. Which one of the following would it be BEST to use to indicate that a file folder has been removed from the files for temporary use in another office?
   A(n)
   A. cross-reference card
   B. tickler file marker
   C. aperture card
   D. out guide

9. Which one of the following is the MOST important objective of filing?
   A. Giving a secretary something to do in her spare time
   B. Making it possible to locate information quickly
   C. Providing a place to store unneeded documents
   D. Keeping extra papers from accumulating on workers' desks

10. If a check has been made out for an incorrect amount, the BEST action for the writer of the check to take is to
    A. erase the original amount and enter the correct amount
    B. cross out the original amount with a single line and enter the correct amount above it
    C. black out the original amount so that it cannot be read and enter the correct amount above it
    D. write a new check

11. Which one of the following BEST describes the usual arrangement of a tickler file? 11.____
    A. Alphabetical   B. Chronological
    C. Numerical   D. Geographical

12. Which one of the following is the LEAST desirable filing practice? 12.____
    A. Using staples to keep papers together
    B. Filing all material without regard to date
    C. Keeping a record of all materials removed from the files
    D. Writing filing instructions on each paper prior to filing

13. Assume that one of your duties is to keep records of the office supplies used by your unit for the purpose of ordering new supplies when the old supplies run out. 13.____
    The information that will be of MOST help in letting you know when to reorder supplies is the
    A. quantity issued   B. quantity received
    C. quantity on hand   D. stock number

Questions 14-19.

DIRECTIONS: Questions 14 through 19 consist of sets of names and addresses. In each question, the name and address in Column II should be an exact copy of the name and address in Column I. If there is
a mistake *only* in the name, mark your answer A;
a mistake *only* in the address, mark your answer B;
a mistake in *both* name and address, mark your answer C;
no mistake in either name or address, mark your answer D.

SAMPLE QUESTION

Column I
Michael Filbert
456 Reade Street
New York, N.Y. 10013

Column II
Michael Filbert
645 Reade Street
New York, N.Y. 10013

Since there is a mistake only in the address (the street number should be 456 instead of 645), the answer to the sample question is B.

COLUMN I   COLUMN II

14. Esta Wong   Esta Wang   14.____
    141 West 68 St.   141 West 68 St.
    New York, N.Y. 10023   New York,, N.Y. 10023

15. Dr. Alberto Grosso   Dr. Alberto Grosso   15.____
    3475 12th Avenue   3475 12th Avenue
    Brooklyn, N.Y. 11218   Brooklyn, N.Y. 11218

4 (#1)

	Column I	Column II	
16.	Mrs. Ruth Bortlas 482 Theresa Ct. Far Rockaway, N.Y. 11691	Ms. Ruth Bortlas 482 Theresa Ct. Far Rockaway, N.Y. 11169	16.____
17.	Mr. and Mrs. Howard Fox 2301 Sedgwick Avenue Bronx, N.Y. 10468	Mr. and Mrs. Howard Fox 231 Sedgwick Ave. Bronx, N.Y. 10458	17.____
18.	Miss Marjorie Black 223 East 23 Street New York, N.Y. 10010	Miss Margorie Black 223 East 23 Street New York, N.Y. 10010	18.____
19.	Michelle Herman 806 Valley Rd. Old Tappan, N.J. 07675	Michelle Hermann 806 Valley Dr. Old Tappan, N.J. 07675	19.____

Questions 20-25.

DIRECTIONS: Questions 20 through 25 are to be answered SOLELY on the basis of the information in the following passage.

Basic to every office is the need for proper lighting. Inadequate lighting is a familiar cause of fatigue and serves to create a somewhat dismal atmosphere in the office. One requirement of proper lighting is that it be of an appropriate intensity. Intensity is measured in foot-candles. According to the Illuminating Engineering Society of New York, for casual seeing tasks such as in reception rooms, inactive file rooms, and other service areas, it is recommended that the amount of light be 30 foot-candles. For ordinary seeing tasks such as reading and work in active file rooms and in mail rooms, the recommended lighting is 100 foot-candles. For very difficult seeing tasks such as accounting, transcribing, and business machine use, the recommended lighting is 150 foot-candles.

Lighting intensity is only one requirement. Shadows and glare are to be avoided. For example, the larger the proportion of a ceiling filled with lighting units, the more glare-free and comfortable the lighting will be. Natural lighting from windows is not too dependable because on dark wintry days, windows yield little usable light, and on sunny afternoons, the glare from windows may be very distracting. Desks should not face the windows. Finally, the main lighting source ought to be overhead and to the left of the user.

20. According to the above passage, insufficient light in the office may cause 20.____
    A. glare   B. shadows   C. tiredness   D. distraction

21. Based on the above passage, which of the following must be considered when 21.____
planning lighting arrangements?
The
    A. amount of natural light present
    B. amount of work to be done
    C. level of difficulty of work to be done
    D. type of activity to be carried out

22. It can be inferred from the above passage that a well-coordinated lighting scheme is LIKELY to result in
    A. greater employee productivity
    B. elimination of light reflection
    C. lower lighting cost
    D. more use of natural light

22.____

23. Of the following, the BEST title for the above passage is
    A. Characteristics of Light
    B. Light Measurement Devices
    C. Factors to Consider When Planning Lighting Systems
    D. Comfort vs. Cost When Devising Lighting Arrangements

23.____

24. According to the above passage, a foot-candle is a measurement of the
    A. number of bulbs used
    B. strength of the light
    C. contrast between glare and shadow
    D. proportion of the ceiling filled with lighting units

24.____

25. According to the above passage, the number of foot-candles of light that would be needed to copy figures onto a payroll is _____ foot-candles.
    A. less than 30   B. 30   C. 100   D. 150

25.____

KEY (CORRECT ANSWERS)

1.	B		11.	B
2.	B		12.	B
3.	B		13.	C
4.	A		14.	A
5.	B		15.	D
6.	A		16.	C
7.	A		17.	B
8.	D		18.	A
9.	B		19.	C
10.	D		20.	C

21.	D
22.	A
23.	C
24.	B
25.	D

TEST 2

DIRECTIONS: Each question or incomplete statement is followed by several suggested answers or completions. Select the one that BEST answers the question or completes the statement. *PRINT THE LETTER OF THE CORRECT ANSWER IN THE SPACE AT THE RIGHT.*

1. Assume that a supervisor has three subordinates who perform clerical tasks. One of the employees retires and is replaced by someone who is transferred from another unit in the agency. The transferred employee tells the supervisor that she has worked as a clerical employee for two years and understands clerical operations quite well. The supervisor then assigns the transferred employee to a desk, tells the employee to begin working, and returns to his own desk.
   The supervisor's action in this situation is
   A. *proper*; experienced clerical employees do not require training when they are transferred to new assignments
   B. *improper*; before the supervisor returns to his desk, he should tell the other two subordinates to watch the transferred employee perform the work
   C. *proper*; if the transferred employee makes any mistakes, she will bring them to the supervisor's attention
   D. *improper*; the supervisor should find out what clerical tasks the transferred employee has performed and give her instruction in those which are new or different

   1.____

2. Assume that you are falling behind in completing your work assignments and you believe that your workload is too heavy.
   Of the following, the BEST course of action for you to take FIRST is to
   A. discuss the problem with your supervisor
   B. decide which of your assignments can be postponed
   C. try to get some of your co-workers to help you out
   D. plan to take some of the work home with you in order to catch up

   2.____

3. Suppose that one of the clerks under your supervision is filling in monthly personnel forms. She asks you to explain a particular personnel regulation which is related to various items on the forms. You are not thoroughly familiar with the regulation.
   Of the following responses you may make, the one which will gain the MOST respect from the clerk and which is generally the MOST advisable is to
   A. tell the clerk to do the best she can and that you will check her work later
   B. inform the clerk that you are not sure of a correct explanation but suggest a procedure for her to follow
   C. give the clerk a suitable interpretation so that she will think you are familiar with all regulations
   D. tell the clerk that you will have to read the regulation more thoroughly before you can give her an explanation

   3.____

4. Charging out records until a specified due date, with prompt follow-up if they 4.____
 are not returned, is a
   A. *good* idea; it may prevent the records from being kept needlessly on someone's desk for long periods of time
   B. *good* idea; it will indicate the extent of your authority to other departments
   C. *poor* idea; the person borrowing the material may make an error because of the pressure put upon him to return the records
   D. *poor* idea; other departments will feel that you do not trust them with the records and they will be resentful

Questions 5-9.

DIRECTIONS: Questions 5 through 9 consist of three lines of code letters and numbers. The numbers on each line should correspond with the code letters on the same line in accordance with the table below.

Code Letter	P	L	I	J	B	O	H	U	C	G
Corresponding Letter	0	1	2	3	4	5	6	7	8	9

On some of the lines, an error exists in the coding. Compare the letters and numbers in each question carefully. If you find an error or errors on
 only one of the lines in the question, mark your answer A;
 any two lines in the question, mark your answer B;
 all three lines in the question, mark your answer C;
 none of the lines in the question, mark your answer D.

SAMPLE QUESTION
JHOILCP   3652180
BICLGUP   4286970
UCIBHLJ   5824613

In the above sample, the first line is correct since each code letter listed has the correct corresponding number. On the second line, an error exists because code letter L should have the number 1 instead of the number 6. On the third line, an error exists because the code letter U should have the number 7 instead of the number 5. Since there are errors on two of the three lines, the correct answer is B.

5. BULJCIP   4713920   5.____
    HIGPOUL   6290571
    OCUHJJBI   5876342

6. CUBLOIJ   8741023   6.____
    LCLGCLB   1818914
    JPUHIOC   3076158

7. OIJGCBPO   52398405   7.____
    UHPBLIOP   76041250
    CLUIPGPC   81720908

8. BPCOUOJI   40875732
    UOHCIPLB   75682014
    GLHUUCBJ   92677843

9. HOIOHJLH   65256361
    IOJJHHBP   25536640
    OJHBJOPI   53642502

Questions 10-13.

DIRECTIONS: Questions 10 through 13 are to be answered SOLELY on the basis of the information given in the following passage.

The mental attitude of the employee toward safety is exceedingly important in preventing accidents. All efforts designed to keep safety on the employee's mind and to keep accident prevention a live subject in the office will help substantially in a safety program. Although it may seem strange, it is common for people to be careless. Therefore, safety education is a continuous process.

Safety rules should be explained, and the reasons for their rigid enforcement should be given to employees. Telling employees to be careful or giving similar general safety warnings and slogans is probably of little value. Employees should be informed of basic safety fundamentals. This can be done through staff meetings, informal suggestions to employees, movies, and safety instruction cards. Safety instruction cards provide the employees with specific suggestions about safety and serve as a series of timely reminder helping to keep safety on the minds of employees. Pictures, posters, and cartoon sketches on bulletin boards that are located in areas continually used by employees arouse the employees' interest in safety. It is usually good to supplement this type of safety promotion with intensive individual follow-up.

10. The above passage implies that the LEAST effective of the following safety measures is
    A. rigid enforcement of safety rules
    B. getting employees to think in terms of safety
    C. elimination of unsafe conditions in the office
    D. telling employees to stay alert at all times

11. The reason given by the passage for maintaining ongoing safety education is that
    A. people are often careless
    B. office tasks are often dangerous
    C. the value of safety slogans increases with repetition
    D. safety rules change frequently

12. Which one of the following safety aids is MOST likely to be preferred by the passage? A
    A. cartoon of a man tripping over a carton and yelling, *Keep aisles clear!*
    B. poster with a large number one and a caption saying, *Safety First*

C. photograph of a very neatly arranged office
D. large sign with the word THINK in capital letters

13. Of the following, the BEST title for the above passage is   13.____
    A. Basic Safety Fundamentals
    B. Enforcing Safety Among Careless Employees
    C. Attitudes Toward Safety
    D. Making Employees Aware of Safety

Questions 14-21.

DIRECTIONS: Questions 14 through 21 are to be answered SOLELY on the basis of the information and chart given below.

The following chart shows expenses in five selected categories for a one-year period, expressed as percentages of these same expenses during the previous year. The chart compares two different offices. In Office T (represented by ▓▓▓▓), a cost reduction program has been tested for the past year. The other office, Office Q (represented by ▨▨▨▨), served as a control, in that no special effort was made to reduce costs during the past year.

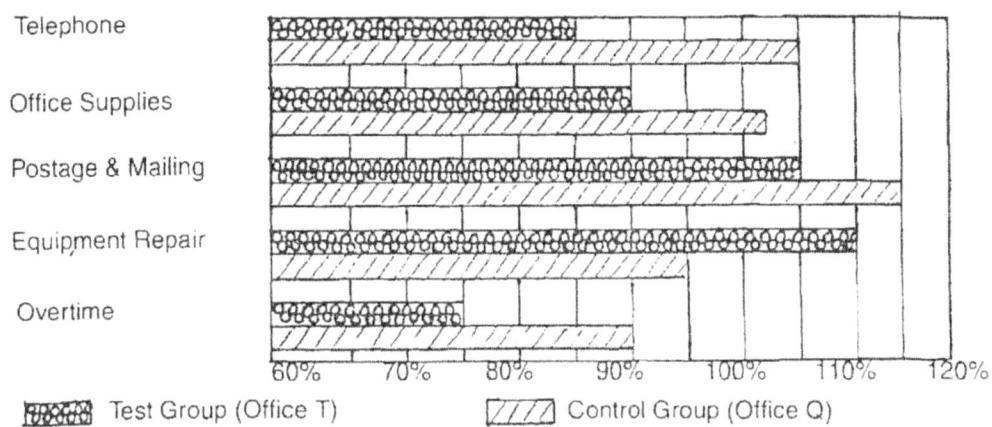

RESULTS OF OFFICE COST REDUCTION PROGRAM
Expenses of Test and Control Groups for 2020
Expressed as Percentages of Same Expenses for 2019

14. In Office T, which category of expense showed the greatest percentage REDUCTION from 2019 to 2020?   14.____
    A. Telephone   B. Office Supplies
    C. Postage & Mailing D. Overtime

15. In which expense category did Office T show the BEST results in percentage terms when compared to Office Q?   15.____
    A. Telephone   B. Office Supplies
    C. Postage & Mailing D. Overtime

5 (#2)

16. According to the above chart, the cost reduction program was LEAST effective for the expense category of 16.____
    A. Office Supplies   B. Postage & Mailing
    C. Equipment Repair   D. Overtime

17. Office T's telephone costs went down during 2020 by approximately how many percentage points? 17.____
    A. 15   B. 20   C. 85   D. 104

18. Which of the following changes occurred in expenses for Office Supplies in Office Q in the year 2020 as compared with the year 2019? 18.____
    They
    A. increased by more than 100%
    B. remained the same
    C. decreased by a few percentage points
    D. increased by a few percentage points

19. For which of the following expense categories do the results in Office T and the results in Office Q differ MOST NEARLYY by 10 percentage points? 19.____
    A. Telephone   B. Postage & Mailing
    C. Equipment Repair   D. Overtime

20. In which expense category did Office Q's costs show the GREATEST percentage increase in 2020? 20.____
    A. Telephone   B. Office Supplies
    C. Postage & Mailing   D. Equipment Repair

21. In Office T, by approximately what percentage did overtime expense change during the past year? It 21.____
    A. *increased* by 15%   B. *increased* by 75%
    C. *decreased* by 10%   D. *decreased* by 25%

22. In a particular agency, there were 160 accidents in 2017. Of these accidents, 75% were due to unsafe acts and the rest were due to unsafe conditions. In the following year, a special safety program was established. The number of accidents in 2019 due to unsafe acts was reduced to 35% of what it had been in 2017. 22.____
    How many accidents due to unsafe acts were there in 2019?
    A. 20   B. 36   C. 42   D. 56

23. At the end of every month, the petty cash fund of Agency A is reimbursed for payments made from the fund during the month. During the month of February, the amounts paid from the fund were entered on receipts as follows: 10 bus fares of $3.50 each and one taxi fare of $35.00. At the end of the month, the money left in the fund was in the following denominations: 15 ten-dollar bills, 10 one-dollar bills, 40 quarters, and 100 dimes. 23.____
    If the petty cash fund is reduced by 20% for the following month, how much money will there be available in the petty cash fund for March?
    A. $110.00   B. $200.00   C. $215.00   D. $250.00

24. The one of the following records which it would be MOST advisable to keep in alphabetical order is a
    A. continuous listing of phone messages, including time and caller, for your supervisor
    B. listing of individuals currently employed by your agency in a particular title
    C. record of purchases paid for by the petty cash fund
    D. dated record of employees who have borrowed material from the files in your office

25. Assume that you have been asked to copy by hand a column of numbers with two decimal places from one record to another. Each number consists of three, four, and five digits.
    In order to copy them quickly and accurately, you should copy
    A. each number exactly, making sure that the column of digits farthest to the right is in a straight line and all other columns are lined up
    B. the column of digits farthest to the right and then copy the next column of digits moving from right to left
    C. the column of digits farthest to the left and then copy the next column of digits moving from left to right
    D. the digits to the right of each decimal point and then copy the digits to the left of each decimal point

KEY (CORRECT ANSWERS)

1.	D		11.	A
2.	A		12.	A
3.	D		13.	D
4.	A		14.	D
5.	A		15.	A
6.	C		16.	C
7.	D		17.	A
8.	B		18.	D
9.	C		19.	B
10.	D		20.	C

21.	D
22.	C
23.	B
24.	B
25.	A

EXAMINATION SECTION
TEST 1

DIRECTIONS: Each question or incomplete statement is followed by several suggested answers or completions. Select the one that BEST answers the question or completes the statement. *PRINT THE LETTER OF THE CORRECT ANSWER IN THE SPACE AT THE RIGHT.*

1. Records of one type or another are kept in every office. The MOST important of the following reasons for the supervisor of a clerical or stenographic unit to keep statistical records of the work done in his unit is generally to

    A. supply basic information needed in planning the work of the unit
    B. obtain statistics for comparison with other units
    C. serve as the basis for unsatisfactory employee evaluation
    D. provide the basis for special research projects on program budgeting

    1.____

2. It is better for an employee to report and be responsible directly to several supervisors than to report and be responsible to only one supervisor.
   This statement directly CONTRADICTS the supervisory principle generally known as

    A. span of control   B. unity of command
    C. delegation of authority D. accountability

    2.____

3. The one of the following which would MOST likely lead to friction among clerks in a unit is for the unit supervisor to

    A. defend the actions of his clerks when discussing them with his own supervisor
    B. praise each of his clerks "in confidence" as the best clerk in the unit
    C. get his men to work together as a team in completing the work of the unit
    D. consider the point of view of the rank and file clerks when assigning unpleasant tasks

    3.____

4. You become aware that one of the employees you supervise has failed to follow correct procedure and has been permitting various reports to be prepared, typed, and transmitted improperly.
   The BEST action for you to take FIRST in this situation is to

    A. order the employee to review all departmental procedures and reprimand him for having violated them
    B. warn the employee that he must obey regulations because uniformity is essential for effective departmental operation
    C. confer with the employee both about his failure to follow regulations and his reasons for doing so
    D. watch the employee's work very closely in the future but say nothing about this violation

    4.____

5. The supervisory clerk who would be MOST likely to have poor control over his subordinates is the one who

    A. goes to unusually great lengths to try to win their approval
    B. pitches in with the work they are doing during periods of heavy workload when no extra help can be obtained

    5.____

C. encourages and helps his subordinates toward advancement
D. considers suggestions from his subordinates before establishing new work procedures involving them

6. Suppose that a clerk who has been transferred to your office from another division in your agency because of difficulties with his supervisor has been placed under your supervision.
The BEST course of action for you to take FIRST is to

   A. instruct the clerk in the duties he will be performing in your office and make him feel "wanted" in his new position
   B. analyze the clerk's past grievance to determine if the transfer was the best solution to the problem
   C. advise him of the difficulties that his former supervisor had with other employees and encourage him not to feel badly about the transfer
   D. warn him that you will not tolerate any nonsense and that he will be under continuous surveillance while assigned to you

7. A certain office supervisor takes the initiative to represent his employees' interests related to working conditions, opportunities for advancement, etc. to his own supervisor and the administrative levels of the agency. This supervisor's actions will MOST probably have the effect of

   A. preventing employees from developing individual initiative in their work goals
   B. encouraging employees to compete openly for the special attention of their supervisor
   C. depriving employees of the opportunity to be represented by persons and/or unions of their own choosing
   D. building employee confidence in their supervisor and a spirit of cooperation in their work

8. Suppose that you have been promoted, assigned as a supervisor of a certain unit and asked to reorganize its functions so that specific routine procedures can be established. Before deciding which routines to establish, the FIRST of the following steps you should take is to

   A. decide who will perform each task in the routine
   B. determine the purpose to be served by each routine procedure
   C. outline the sequence of steps in each routine to be established
   D. calculate if more staff will be needed to carry out the new procedures

9. When routine procedures covering the ordinary work of an office are established, the supervisor of the office tends to be relieved of the need to

   A. make repeated decisions on the handling of recurring similar situations
   B. check the accuracy of the work completed by his subordinates
   C. train his subordinates in new work procedures
   D. plan and schedule the work of his office

10. Of the following, the method which would be LEAST helpful to a supervisor in effectively applying the principles of on-the-job safety to the daily work of his unit is for him to

A. initiate corrections of unsafe layouts of equipment and unsafe work processes
B. take charge of operations that are not routine to make certain that safety precautions are established and observed
C. continue to "talk safety" and promote safety consciousness in his subordinates
D. figure the cost of all accidents which could possibly occur on the job

11. A clerk is assigned to serve as receptionist for a large and busy office. Although many members of the public visit this office, the clerk often experiences periods of time in which he has nothing to do.
    In these circumstances, the MOST advisable of the following actions for the supervisor to take is to

    A. assign a number of relatively low priority clerical jobs to the receptionist to do in the slow periods
    B. regularly rotate this assignment so that all the clerks experience this lighter work load
    C. assign the receptionist job as part of the duties of a number of clerks whose desks are nearest the reception room
    D. overlook the situation, since most of the receptionist's time is spent in performing a necessary and meaningful function

12. For a supervisor to require all stenographers in a stenographic pool to produce the same amount of work on a particular day is

    A. *advisable;* since it will prove that the supervisor plays no favorites
    B. *fair;* since all the stenographers are receiving approximately the same salary, their output should be equivalent
    C. *not necessary;* since the fast workers will compensate for the slow workers
    D. *not realistic;* since individual differences in abilities and work assignment must be taken into consideration

13. The establishment of a centralized typing pool to service the various units in an organization is MOST likely to be worthwhile when there is

    A. wide fluctuation from time to time in the needs of the various units for typing service
    B. a large volume of typing work to be done in each of the units
    C. a need by each unit for different kinds of typing service
    D. a training program in operation to develop and maintain typing skills

14. A newly appointed supervisor should learn as much as possible about the backgrounds of his subordinates. This statement is generally CORRECT because

    A. knowing their backgrounds assures they will be treated objectively, equally, and without favor
    B. effective handling of subordinates is based upon knowledge of their individual differences
    C. subordinates perform more efficiently under one supervisor than under another
    D. subordinates have confidence in a supervisor who knows all about them

15. The use of electronic computers in modern businesses has produced many changes in office and information management. Of the following, it would NOT be correct to state that computer utilization

A. broadens the scope of managerial and supervisory authority
B. establishes uniformity in the processing and reporting of information
C. cuts costs by reducing the personnel needed for efficient office operation
D. supplies management rapidly with up-to-date data to facilitate decision-making

16. The CHIEF advantage of having a single, large open office instead of small partitioned ones for a clerical unit or stenographic pool is that the single, large open office

   A. affords privacy without isolation for all office workers not directly dealing with the public
   B. assures the smoother, more continuous inter-office flow of work that is essential for efficient work production
   C. facilitates the office supervisor's visual control over and communication with his subordinates
   D. permits a more decorative and functional arrangement of office furniture and machines

17. When a supervisor provides a new employee with the information necessary for a basic knowledge and a general understanding of practices and procedures of the agency, he is applying the type of training generally known as _____ training.

   A. pre-employment   B. induction
   C. on-the-job   D. supervisory

18. Many government agencies require the approval by a central forms control unit of the design and reproduction of new office forms.
   The one of the following results of this procedure that is a DISADVANTAGE is that requiring prior approval of a central forms control unit USUALLY

   A. limits the distribution of forms to those offices with justifiable reasons for receiving them
   B. permits checking whether existing forms or modifications of them are in line with current agency needs
   C. encourages reliance on only the central office to set up all additional forms when needed
   D. provides for someone with a specialized knowledge of forms design to review and criticize new and revised forms

19. Suppose that a large quantity of information is in the files which are located a good distance from your desk. Almost every worker in your office must use these files constantly. Your duties in particular require that you daily refer to about 25 of the same items. They are short, one-page items distributed throughout the files.
   In this situation, your BEST course would be to

   A. take the items that you use daily from the files and keep them on your desk, inserting "out cards" in their place
   B. go to the files each time you need the information so that the items will be there when other workers need them
   C. make xerox copies of the information you use most frequently and keep them in your desk for ready reference
   D. label the items you use most often with different colored tabs for immediate identification

20. Of the following, the MOST important advantage of preparing manuals of office procedures in loose-leaf form is that this form

   A. permits several employees to use different sections simultaneously
   B. facilitates the addition of new material and the removal of obsolete material
   C. is more readily arranged in alphabetical order
   D. reduces the need for cross-references to locate material carried under several headings

21. Suppose that you establish a new clerical procedure for the unit you supervise. Your keeping a close check on the time required by your staff to handle the new procedure is wise MAINLY because such a check will find out

   A. whether your subordinates know how to handle the new procedure
   B. whether a revision of the unit's work schedule will be necessary as a result of the new procedure
   C. what attitude your employees have toward the new procedure
   D. what alterations in job descriptions will be necessitated by the new procedure

22. From the viewpoint of an office supervisor, the BEST of the following reasons for distributing the incoming mail *before* the beginning of the regular work day is that

   A. distribution can be handled quickly and most efficiently at that time
   B. distribution later in the day may be distracting to or interfere with other employees
   C. the employees who distribute the mail can then perform other tasks during the rest of the day
   D. office activities for the day based on the mail may then be started promptly

23. Suppose you are the head of a unit with ten staff members who are located in several different rooms. If you want to inform your staff of a *minor* change in procedure, the BEST and LEAST expensive way of doing so would usually be to

   A. send a mimeographed copy to each staff member
   B. call a special staff meeting and announce the change
   C. circulate a memo, having each staff member initial it
   D. have a clerk tell each member of the staff about the change

24. The numbered statements below relate to the stenographic skill of taking dictation. According to authorities on secretarial practices, which of these are GENERALLY recommended guides to development of efficient stenographic skills?
   A stenographer should

   I. date her notebook daily to facilitate locating certain notes at a later time
   II. make corrections of grammatical mistakes while her boss is dictating to her
   III. draw a line through the dictated matter in her notebook after she has transcribed it
   IV. write in longhand unfamiliar names and addresses dictated to her

   The CORRECT answer is:

   A. I, II, III   B. II, III, IV
   C. I, III, IV   D. All of the above

25. A bureau of a city agency is about to move to a new location.
    Of the following, the FIRST step that should be taken in order to provide a good layout for the office at the new location is to

A. decide the exact amount of space to be assigned to each unit of the bureau
B. decide whether to lay out a single large open office or one consisting of small partitioned units
C. ask each unit chief in the bureau to examine the new location and submit a request for the amount of space he needs
D. prepare a detailed plan of the dimensions of the floor space to be occupied by the bureau at the new location

KEY (CORRECT ANSWERS)

1. A
2. B
3. B
4. C
5. A

6. A
7. D
8. B
9. A
10. D

11. A
12. D
13. A
14. B
15. A

16. C
17. B
18. C
19. C
20. B

21. B
22. D
23. C
24. C
25. D

TEST 2

DIRECTIONS: Each question or incomplete statement is followed by several suggested answers or completions. Select the one that BEST answers the question or completes the statement. *PRINT THE LETTER OF THE CORRECT ANSWER IN THE SPACE AT THE RIGHT.*

1. Suppose you are the supervisor of the mailroom of a large agency where the mail received daily is opened by machine, sorted by hand for delivery and time-stamped. Letters and any enclosures are removed from envelopes and stapled together before distribution. One of your newest clerks asks you what should be done when a letter makes reference to an enclosure, but no enclosure is in the envelope.
   You should tell him that in this situation the BEST procedure is to

   A. make an entry of the sender's name and address in the "missing enclosures" file and forward the letter to its proper destination
   B. return the letter to its sender, attaching a request for the missing enclosure
   C. put the letter aside until a proper investigation may be made concerning the missing enclosure
   D. route the letter to the person for whom it is intended, noting the absence of the enclosure on the letter margin

2. The term "work flow," when used in connection with office management or the activities in an office, GENERALLY means the

   A. use of charts in the analysis of various office functions
   B. rate of speed at which work flows through a single section of an office
   C. step-by-step physical routing of work through its various procedures
   D. number of individual work units which can be produced by the average employee

3. Physical conditions can have a definite effect on the efficiency and morale of an office. Which of the following statements about physical conditions in an office is CORRECT?

   A. Hard, non-porous surfaces reflect more noise than linoleum on the top of a desk.
   B. Painting in tints of bright yellow is more appropriate for sunny, well-lit offices than for dark, poorly-lit offices.
   C. Plate glass is better than linoleum for the top of a desk.
   D. The central typing room needs less light than a conference room does.

4. In a certain filing system, documents are consecutively numbered as they are filed, a register is maintained of such consecutively numbered documents, and a record is kept of the number of each document removed from the files and its destination.
   This system will NOT help in

   A. finding the present whereabouts of a particular document
   B. proving the accuracy of the data recorded on a certain document
   C. indicating whether observed existing documents were ever filed
   D. locating a desired document without knowing what its contents are

5. In deciding the kind and number of records an agency should keep, the administrative staff must recognize that records are of value in office management PRIMARILY as

A. informational bases for agency activities
B. data for evaluating the effectiveness of the agency
C. raw material on which statistical analyses are to be based
D. evidence that the agency is carrying out its duties and responsibilities

6. Complaints are often made by the public about the city government's procedures. Although in most cases such procedures cannot be changed since various laws and regulations require them, it may still be possible to reduce the number of complaints. Which one of the following actions by personnel dealing with applicants for city services is LEAST likely to reduce complaints concerning city procedures?

    A. Treating all citizens alike and explaining to them that no exceptions to required procedures can be made
    B. Explaining briefly to the citizen why he should comply with regulations
    C. Being careful to avoid mistakes which may make additional interviews or correspondence necessary
    D. Keeping the citizen informed of the progress of his correspondence when immediate disposition cannot be made

7. In answering a complaint made by a member of the public that a certain essential procedure required by your agency is difficult to follow, it would be BEST for you to stress MOST

    A. that a change in the rules may be considered if enough complaints are received
    B. why the operation of a large agency sometimes proves a hardship in individual cases
    C. the necessity for the procedure
    D. the origin of the procedure

8. When talking to a citizen, it is BEST for an employee of government to

    A. use ordinary conversational phrases and a natural manner
    B. try to copy the pronunciation and level of education shown by the citizen
    C. try to speak in a very cultured manner and tone
    D. use technical terms to show his familiarity with his own work

9. Employees who service the public should maintain an attitude which is both sympathetic and objective.
An UNSYMPATHETIC and SUBJECTIVE attitude would be shown by a public employee who

    A. says "no" with a smile when a citizen's request must be denied
    B. listens attentively to a long complaint from a citizen about the government's "red tape"
    C. responds with sarcasm when a citizen asks a question which has an obvious answer
    D. suggests a definite solution to a citizen's problems

10. You are a supervisor in a city agency and are holding your first interview with a new employee.
In this interview, you should strive MAINLY to

A. show the new employee that you are an efficient and objective supervisor, with a completely impersonal attitude toward your subordinates
B. complete the entire orientation process including the giving of detailed job-duty instructions
C. make it clear to the employee that all your decisions are based on your many years of experience
D. lay the groundwork for a good employee-supervisor relationship by gaining the new employee's confidence

11. A senior clerk or senior typist may be required to help train a newly-appointed clerk. Which of the following is LEAST important for a newly-appointed clerk to know in order to perform his work efficiently? 11.____

   A. Acceptable ways of answering and recording telephone calls
   B. The number of files in the storage files unit
   C. The filing methods used by his unit
   D. Proper techniques for handling visitors

12. In your agency, you have the responsibility of processing clients who have appointments with agency representatives. On a particularly busy day, a client comes to your desk and insists that she must see the person handling her case although she has no appointment.
    Under the circumstances, your FIRST action should be to 12.____

   A. show her the full appointment schedule
   B. give her an appointment for another day
   C. ask her to explain the urgency
   D. tell her to return later in the day

13. Which of the following practices is BEST for a supervisor to use when assigning work to his staff? 13.____

   A. Give workers with seniority the most difficult jobs
   B. Assign all unimportant work to the slower workers
   C. Permit each employee to pick the job he prefers
   D. Make assignments based on the workers' abilities

14. In which of the following instances is a supervisor MOST justified in giving commands to people under his supervision? When 14.____

   A. they delay in following instructions which have been given to them clearly
   B. they become relaxed and slow about work, and he wants to speed up their production
   C. he must direct them in an emergency situation
   D. he is instructing them on jobs that are unfamiliar to them

15. Which of the following supervisory actions or attitudes is MOST likely to result in getting subordinates to try to do as much work as possible for a supervisor? He 15.____

   A. shows that his most important interest is in schedules and production goals
   B. consistently pressures his staff to get the work out
   C. never fails to let them know he is in charge
   D. considers their abilities and needs while requiring that production goals be met

16. Assume that a senior clerk has been explaining certain regulations to a new clerk under his supervision.
    The MOST efficient way for the senior clerk to make sure that the clerk has understood the explanation is to

    A. give him written materials on the regulations
    B. ask him if he has any further questions about the regulations
    C. ask him specific questions based on what has just been explained to him
    D. watch the way he handles a situation involving these regulations

17. One of your unit clerks has been assigned to work for a Mr. Jones in another office for several days. At the end of the first day, Mr. Jones, saying the clerk was not satisfactory, asks that she not be assigned to him again. This clerk is one of your most dependable workers, and no previous complaints about her work have come to you from any other outside assignments.
    To get to the root of this situation, your FIRST action should be to

    A. ask Mr. Jones to explain in what way her work was unsatisfactory
    B. ask the clerk what she did that Mr. Jones considered unsatisfactory
    C. check with supervisors for whom she previously worked to see if your own rating of her is in error
    D. tell Mr. Jones to pick the clerk he would prefer to have work for him the next time

18. A senior typist, still on probation, is instructed to type, as quickly as possible, one section of a draft of a long, complex report. Her part must be typed and readable before another part of the report can be written. Asked when she can have the report ready, she gives her supervisor an estimate of a day longer than she knows it will actually take. She then finishes the job a day sooner than the date given her supervisor.
    The judgment shown by a senior typist in giving an overestimate of time in a situation like this is, in general,

    A. *good,* because it prevents the supervisor from thinking she works slowly
    B. *good,* because it keeps unrealistic supervisors from expecting too much
    C. *bad,* because she should have used the time left to further check and proofread her work
    D. *bad,* because schedules and plans for other parts of the project may have been based on her false estimate

19. Suppose a new clerk, still on probation, is placed under your supervision and refuses to do a job you ask him to do.
    What is the FIRST thing you should do?

    A. Explain that you are the supervisor, and he must follow your instructions.
    B. Tell him he may be suspended if he refuses.
    C. Ask someone else to do the job, and rate him accordingly.
    D. Ask for his reason for objecting to the request.

20. As a supervisor of a small group of people, you have blamed worker A for something that you later find out was really done by worker B.
    The BEST thing for you to do now would be to

    A. say nothing to worker A, but criticize worker B for his mistake while worker A is near so that A will realize that you know who made the mistake
    B. speak to each worker separately, apologize to worker A for your mistake, and discuss worker B's mistake with him
    C. bring both workers together, apologize to worker A for your mistake, and discuss worker B's mistake with him
    D. say nothing new but be careful about mixing up worker A with worker B in the future

21. You have just learned one of your staff is grumbling that she thinks you are not pleased with her work. As far as you are concerned, this is not true at all. In fact, you have paid no particular attention to this worker lately because you have been very busy. You have just finished preparing an important report and "breaking in" a new clerk.
    Under the circumstances, the BEST thing to do is

    A. ignore her; after all, it is just a figment of her imagination
    B. discuss the matter with her now to try to find out and eliminate the cause of this problem
    C. tell her not to worry about it; you have not had time to think about her work
    D. make a note to meet with her at a later date in order to straighten out the situation

22. A most important job of a supervisor is to positively motivate employees to increase their work production. Which of the following LEAST indicates that a group of workers has been positively motivated?

    A. Their work output becomes constant and stable.
    B. Their cooperation at work becomes greater.
    C. They begin to show pride in the product of their work.
    D. They show increased interest in their work.

23. Which of the following traits would be LEAST important in considering a person for a merit increase?

    A. Punctuality
    B. Using initiative successfully
    C. High rate of production
    D. Resourcefulness

24. Of the following, the action LEAST likely to gain a supervisor the cooperation of his staff is for him to

    A. give each person consideration as an individual
    B. be as objective as possible when evaluating work performance
    C. rotate the least popular assignments
    D. expect subordinates to be equally competent

25. It has been said that, for the supervisor, nothing can beat the "face-to-face" communication of talking to one subordinate at a time.
This method is, however, LEAST appropriate to use when the

   A. supervisor is explaining a change in general office procedure
   B. subject is of personal importance
   C. supervisor is conducting a yearly performance evaluation of all employees
   D. supervisor must talk to some of his employees concerning their poor attendance and punctuality

---

KEY (CORRECT ANSWERS)

1.	D	11.	B
2.	C	12.	C
3.	A	13.	D
4.	B	14.	C
5.	A	15.	D
6.	A	16.	C
7.	C	17.	A
8.	A	18.	D
9.	C	19.	D
10.	D	20.	B

21. B
22. A
23. A
24. D
25. A

TEST 3

DIRECTIONS: Each question or incomplete statement is followed by several suggested answers or completions. Select the one that BEST answers the question or completes the statement. *PRINT THE LETTER OF THE CORRECT ANSWER IN THE SPACE AT THE RIGHT.*

1. While you are on the telephone answering a question about your agency, a visitor comes to your desk and starts to ask you a question. There is no emergency or urgency in either situation, that of the phone call or that of answering the visitor's question.
   In this case, you should

   A. continue to answer the person on the telephone until you are finished and then tell the visitor you are sorry to have kept him waiting
   B. excuse yourself to the person on the telephone and tell the visitor that you will be with him as soon as you have finished on the phone
   C. explain to the person on the telephone that you have a visitor and must shorten the conversation
   D. continue to answer the person on the phone while looking up occasionally at the visitor to let him know that you know he is waiting

   1.____

2. While speaking on the telephone to someone who called, you are disconnected.
   The FIRST thing you should do is

   A. hang up, but try to keep your line free to receive the call back
   B. immediately get the dial tone and continually dial the person who called you until you reach him
   C. signal the switchboard operator and ask her to re-establish the connection
   D. dial "O" for Operator and explain that you were disconnected

   2.____

3. The type of speech used by an office worker in telephone conversation greatly affects the communication.
   Of the following, the BEST way to express your ideas when telephoning is with a vocabulary that consists MAINLY of

   A. formal, intellectual sounding words
   B. often used colloquial words
   C. technical, emphatic words
   D. simple, descriptive words

   3.____

4. Suppose a clerk under your supervision has taken a personal phone call and is at the same time needed to answer a question regarding an assignment being handled by another member of your office. He appears confused as to what he should do. How should you instruct him later as to how to handle a similar situation?
   You should tell him to

   A. tell the caller to hold on while he answers the question
   B. tell the caller to call back a little later
   C. return the call during an assigned break
   D. finish the conversation quickly and answer the question

   4.____

5. You are asked to place a telephone call by your supervisor. When you place the call, you receive what appears to be a wrong number.
   Of the following, you should FIRST

   A. check the number with your supervisor to see if the number he gave you is correct
   B. ask the person on the other end what his number is and who he is
   C. check with the person on the other end to see if the number you dialed is the number you received
   D. apologize to the person on the other end for disturbing him and hang up

6. When you select someone to serve as supervisor of your unit during your absence on vacation and at other times, it would generally be BEST to choose the employee who is

   A. able to move the work along smoothly, without friction
   B. on staff longest
   C. liked best by the rest of the staff
   D. able to perform the work of each employee to be supervised

7. Successful supervision of handicapped persons employed in a department depends MOST on providing them with a work place and work climate

   A. which is safe and accident-free
   B. that requires close and direct supervision by others
   C. that requires the performance of routine, repetitive tasks under a minimum of pressure
   D. where they will be accepted by the other employees

8. Studies have indicated that when employees feel that their work is aimless and unchallenging, the allocation or payment of more money for this type of work is likely to

   A. contribute little to increased production
   B. bring more status to this work
   C. increase employees' feelings of security
   D. give employees greater motivation

9. An employee's performance has fallen below established minimum standards of quantity and quality.
   The threat of monetary or other disciplinary action as a device for improving this employee's performance would probably be acceptable and MOST effective

   A. only if applied as soon as the performance fell below standard
   B. only after more constructive techniques have failed
   C. at any time provided the employee understands that the punishment will be carried out
   D. at no time

10. A supervisor must, on short notice, ask his staff to work overtime.
    Of the following, a technique that is MOST likely to win their willing cooperation would be to

    A. explain that occasional overtime is part of the job requirement
    B. explain that they will be doing him a personal favor which he will appreciate very much

C. explain why the overtime is necessary
D. promise them that they can take the extra time off in the near future

11. On checking a completed work assignment of an employee, the supervisor finds that the work was not done correctly because the employee had not understood his instructions. Of the following, the BEST way to prevent repetition of this situation next time is for the supervisor to

    A. ask the employee whether he fully understood the instructions and tell him to ask questions in the future whenever anything is unclear
    B. ask the employee to repeat the instructions given and test his understanding with several key questions
    C. give the instructions a second time, emphasizing the more complicated aspects of the job
    D. give work instructions in writing

12. If, as a supervisor, you find yourself pressured for time to handle all of your job responsibilities, the one of the following tasks which it would be MOST appropriate for you to delegate to a subordinate is

    A. attending a staff conference of unit supervisors to discuss the implementation of a new departmental policy
    B. making staff work assignments
    C. interviewing a new employee
    D. checking work of certain employees for accuracy

13. Suppose you are unavoidably late for work one morning. When you arrive at 10 o'clock, you find there are several matters demanding your attention.
    Which one of the following matters should you handle LAST?

    A. A visitor who had a 9:30 appointment with you has been waiting to see you since 9 o'clock.
    B. An employee on an assignment which should have been completed that morning is absent, and the work will have to be reassigned.
    C. Several letters which you dictated at the end of the previous day have been typed and are on your desk for signature and mailing.
    D. Your superior called asking you to get certain information for him when you come in and to call him back.

14. Suppose that you have assigned a typist to type a report containing considerable statistical and tabular material and have given her specific instructions as to how this material is to be laid out on each page. When she returns the completed report, you find that it was not prepared according to your instructions, but you may possibly be able to use it the way it was typed. When you question her, she states that she thought her layout was better but you were unavailable for consultation when she began the work.
    Of the following, the BEST action for you to take is to

    A. criticize her for not doing the work according to your instructions
    B. have her retype the report
    C. praise her for her work but tell her she should have waited until she could consult you
    D. praise her for using initiative

15. Of the following, the MOST effective way for a supervisor to correct poor work habits of an employee which result in low and poor quality output is to give the employee

    A. additional training
    B. less demanding assignments until his work improves
    C. continuous supervision
    D. more severe criticism

16. Of the following, the BEST way for a supervisor to teach an employee how to do a new and somewhat complicated job is to

    A. assign him to observe another employee who is already skilled in this work and instruct him to consult this employee if he has any questions
    B. explain to him how to do it, then demonstrate how it is done, then observe and correct the employee as he does it, then follow up
    C. give him a written, detailed, step-by-step explanation of how to do the job and instruct him to ask questions if anything is unclear when he does the work
    D. teach him the easiest part of the job first, then the other parts one at a time, in order of their difficulty, as the employee masters the easier parts

17. After an employee has completed telling his supervisor about a grievance against a co-worker, the supervisor tells the employee that he will take action to remove the cause of the grievance.
    The action of the supervisor was

    A. *good,* because ill feeling between subordinates interferes with proper performance
    B. *poor,* because the supervisor should give both employees time to "cool off"
    C. *good,* because grievances that appear petty to the supervisor are important to subordinates
    D. *poor,* because the supervisor should tell the employee that he will investigate the matter before he comes to any conclusion

18. During work on an important project, one employee in a secretarial pool turns in several pages of typed copy, one page of which contains several errors.
    Of these four comments which her supervisor might possibly make, which one would be MOST constructive?

    A. "You did such a poor job on this; I will have to have it done over."
    B. "You will have to do better, more consistently than this, if you want to be in charge of a secretarial pool yourself someday."
    C. "How come you made so many mistakes here? Your other pages were all right."
    D. "If my boss saw this, he would be very displeased with you."

19. A supervisor has general supervision over a large, complex project with many employees. The work is subdivided among small units of employees, each with a senior clerk or senior stenographer in charge. At a staff meeting, after all work assignments have been made, the supervisor tells all the employees that they are to take orders only from their immediate supervisor and instructs them to let him know if anyone else tries to give them orders.
    This instruction by the supervising clerk is

A. *good,* because it may prevent the issuance of orders by unauthorized persons, which would interfere with the accomplishment of the assignment
B. *poor,* because employees should be instructed to take up such problems with their immediate supervisor
C. *good,* because orders issued by immediate supervisors would be precise and directly related to the tasks of the assignments while those issued by others would not be
D. *poor,* because it places upon all employees a responsibility which should not normally be theirs

20. A supervisor who is to direct a team of senior clerks and clerks in a complex project, calls them together beforehand to inform them of the tasks each employee will perform on this job.
Of the following, the CHIEF value of this action by the supervisor is that each member of this team will be able to

    A. work independently in the absence of the supervisor
    B. understand what he will do and how this will fit into the total picture
    C. share in the process of decision-making as an equal participant
    D. judge how well the plans for this assignment have been made

21. A supervisor who has both younger and older employees under his supervision may sometimes find that employee absenteeism seriously interferes with accomplishment of goals.
Studies of such employee absenteeism have shown that the absences of employees

    A. under 35 years of age are usually unexpected and the absences of employees over 45 years of age are usually unnecessary
    B. of all age groups show the same characteristics as to length of absence
    C. under 35 years of age are for frequent, short periods while the absences of employees over 45 years of age are less frequent but of longer duration
    D. under 35 years of age are for periods of long duration and the absences of employees over 45 years of age are for periods of short duration

22. Suppose you have a long-standing procedure for getting a certain job done by your subordinates that is apparently a good one. Changes in some steps of the procedure are made from time to time to handle special problems that come up.
For you to review this procedure periodically is desirable MAINLY because

    A. the system is working well
    B. checking routines periodically is a supervisor's chief responsibility
    C. subordinates may be confused as to how the procedure operates as a result of the changes made
    D. it is necessary to determine whether the procedure has become outdated or is in need of improvement

23. Suppose that a stranger enters the office you are in charge of and asks for the address and telephone number of one of your employees.
Of the following, it would be BEST for you to

    A. find out why he needs the information and release it if his reason is a good one
    B. explain that you are not permitted to release such information to unauthorized persons

C. give him the information but tell him it must be kept confidential
D. ask him to leave the office immediately

24. A member of the public approaches an employee who is at work at his desk. The employee cannot interrupt his work in order to take care of this person.
Of the following, the BEST and MOST courteous way of handling this situation is for the employee to

   A. avoid looking up from his work until he is finished with what he is doing
   B. tell this person that he will not be able to take care of him for quite a while
   C. refer the individual to another employee who can take care of him right away
   D. chat with the individual while he continues with his work

25. You answer a phone call from a citizen who urgently needs certain information you do not have, but you think you know who may have it. He is angry because he has already been switched to two different offices.
Of the following, it would be BEST for you to

   A. give him the phone number of the person you think may have the information he wants, but explain you are not sure
   B. tell him you regret you cannot help him because you are not sure who can give him the information
   C. advise him that the best way he can be sure of getting the information he wants is to write a letter to the agency
   D. get the phone number where he can be reached and tell him you will try to get the information he wants and will call him back later

KEY (CORRECT ANSWERS)

1.	B	11.	B
2.	A	12.	D
3.	D	13.	C
4.	C	14.	A
5.	C	15.	A
6.	A	16.	B
7.	D	17.	D
8.	A	18.	C
9.	B	19.	B
10.	C	20.	B

21. C
22. D
23. B
24. C
25. D

CLERICAL ABILITIES TEST
EXAMINATION SECTION
TEST 1

DIRECTIONS: Each question or incomplete statement is followed by several suggested answers or completions. Select the one that BEST answers the question or completes the statement. *PRINT THE LETTER OF THE CORRECT ANSWER IN THE SPACE AT THE RIGHT.*

Questions 1-10.

DIRECTIONS: Questions 1 through 10 consist of lines of names, dates, and numbers. For each question, you are to choose the option (A, B, C, or D) in Column II which EXACTLY matches the information in Column I. *PRINT THE LETTER OF THE CORRECT ANSWER IN THE SPACE AT THE RIGHT.*

SAMPLE QUESTION

Column I
Schneider 11/16/75 581932

Column II
A. Schneider 11/16/75 518932
B. Schneider 11/16/75 581932
C. Schnieder 11/16/75 581932
D. Shnieder   11/16/75 518932

The correct answer is B. Only Option B shows the name, date, and number exactly as they are in Column I. Option A has a mistake in the number. Option C has a mistake in the name. Option D has a mistake in the name and in the number. Now answer Questions 1 through 10 in the same manner.

Column I
1. Johnston 12/26/74 659251

Column II
A. Johnson   12/23/74 659251
B. Johston   12/26/74 659251
C. Johnston 12/26/74 695251
D. Johnston 12/26/74 659251

1.____

2. Allison 1/26/75 9939256

A. Allison 1/26/75 9939256
B. Alisson 1/26/75 9939256
C. Allison 1/26/76 9399256
D. Allison 1/26/75 9993356

2.____

3. Farrell 2/12/75 361251

A. Farell   2/21/75 361251
B. Farrell 2/12/75 361251
C. Farrell 2/21/75 361251
D. Farrell 2/12/75 361151

3.____

4. Guerrero 4/28/72 105689
    A. Guererro 4/28/72 105689
    B. Guererro 4/28/72 105986
    C. Guererro 4/28/72 105869
    D. Guerrero 4/28/72 105689

    4.____

5. McDonnell 6/05/73 478215
    A. McDonnell 6/15/73 478215
    B. McDonnell 6/05/73 478215
    C. McDonnell 6/05/73 472815
    D. MacDonell 6/05/73 478215

    5.____

6. Shepard 3/31/71 075421
    A. Sheperd 3/31/71 075421
    B. Shepard 3/13/71 075421
    C. Shepard 3/31/71 075421
    D. Shepard 3/13/71 075241

    6.____

7. Russell 4/01/69 031429
    A. Russell 4/01/69 031429
    B. Russell 4/10/69 034129
    C. Russell 4/10/69 031429
    D. Russell 4/01/69 034129

    7.____

8. Phillips 10/16/68 961042
    A. Philipps 10/16/68 961042
    B. Phillips 10/16/68 960142
    C. Phillips 10/16/68 961042
    D. Philipps 10/16/68 916042

    8.____

9. Campbell 11/21/72 624856
    A. Campbell 11/21/72 624856
    B. Campbell 11/21/72 624586
    C. Campbell 11/21/72 624686
    D. Campbel 11/21/72 624856

    9.____

10. Patterson 9/18/71 76199176
    A. Patterson 9/18/72 76191976
    B. Patterson 9/18/71 76199176
    C. Patterson 9/18/72 76199176
    D. Patterson 9/18/71 76919176

    10.____

Questions 11-15.

DIRECTIONS: Questions 11 through 15 consist of groups of numbers and letters which you are to compare. For each question, you are to choose the option (A, B, C, or D) in Column I which EXACTLY matches the group of numbers and letters given in Column I.

SAMPLE QUESTION

Column I
B92466

Column II
A. B92644
B. B94266
C. A92466
D. B92466

The correct answer is D. Only Option D in Column II shows the group of numbers and letters EXACTLY as it appears in Column I. Now answer Questions 11 through 15 in the same manner.

Column I	Column II

11. 925AC5
   A. 952CA5
   B. 925AC5
   C. 952AC5
   D. 925CA6

11.____

12. Y006925
   A. Y060925
   B. Y006295
   C. Y006529
   D. Y006925

12.____

13. J236956
   A. J236956
   B. J326965
   C. J239656
   D. J932656

13.____

14. AB6952
   A. AB6952
   B. AB9625
   C. AB9652
   D. AB6925

14.____

15. X259361
   A. X529361
   B. X259631
   C. X523961
   D. X259361

15.____

Questions 16-25.

DIRECTIONS: Each of questions 16 through 25 consists of three lines of code letters and three lines of numbers. The numbers on each line should correspond with the code letters on the same line in accordance with the table below.

Code Letter	S	V	W	A	Q	M	X	E	G	K
Corresponding Number	0	1	2	3	4	5	5	7	8	9

On some of the lines, an error exists in the coding. Compare the letters and numbers in each question carefully. If you find an error or errors on:
  only one of the lines in the question, mark your answer A;
  any two lines in the question, mark your answer B;
  all three lines in the question, mark your answer C;
  none of the lines in the question, mark your answer D.

SAMPLE QUESTION

WQGKSXG	2489068
XEKVQMA	6591453
KMAESXV	9527061

In the above sample, the first line is correct since each code letter listed has the correct corresponding number. On the second line, an error exists because code letter E should have the number 7 instead of the number 5. On the third line, an error exists because the code letter A should have the number 3 instead of the number 2. Since there are errors in two of the three lines, the correct answer is B. Now answer Questions 16 through 25 in the same manner.

16. SWQEKGA   0247983   16.____
     KEAVSXM   9731065
     SSAXGKQ   0036894

17. QAMKMVS   4259510   17.____
     MGGEASX   5897306
     KSWMKWS   9125920

18. WKXQWVE   2964217   18.____
     QKXXQVA   4966413
     AWMXGVS   3253810

19. GMMKASE   8559307   19.____
     AWVSKSW   3210902
     QAVSVGK   4310189

20. XGKQSMK   6894049   20.____
     QSVKEAS   4019730
     GSMXKMV   8057951

21. AEKMWSG   3195208   21.____
     MKQSVQK   5940149
     XGQAEVW   6843712

22. XGMKAVS   6858310   22.____
     SKMAWEQ   0953174
     GVMEQSA   8167403

23. VQSKAVE   1489317   23.____
     WQGKAEM   2489375
     MEGKAWQ   5689324

24. XMQVSKG   6541098   24.____
     QMEKEWS   4579720
     KMEVGKG   9571983

25. GKVAMEW   88912572   25.____
     AXMVKAE   3651937
     KWAGMAV   9238531

Questions 26-35.

DIRECTIONS: Each of Questions 26 through 35 consists of a column of figures. For each question, add the column of figures and choose the correct answer from the four choices given.

26. 5,665.43   26.____
     2,356.69
     6,447.24
     7,239.65

     A. 20,698.01   B. 21,709.01
     C. 21,718.01   D. 22,609.01

27. 817,209.55   27.____
     264,354.29
      82,368.76
     849,964.89

     A. 1,893.977.49   B. 1,989,988.39
     C. 2,009,077.39   D. 2,013,897.49

28. 156,366.89   28.____
     249,973.23
     823,229.49
      56,869.45

     A. 1,286,439.06   B. 1,287,521.06
     C. 1,297,539.06   D. 1,296,421.06

29.   23,422.15   29.____
     149,696.24
     238,377.53
      86,289.79
     505,533.63

     A. 989,229.34   B. 999,879.34
     C. 1,003,330.34   D. 1,023,329.34

30. 2,468,926.70
    656,842.28
    49,723.15
    832,369.59

    A. 3,218,062.72 B. 3,808,092.72
    C. 4,007,861.72 D. 4,818,192.72

31. 524,201.52
    7,775,678.51
    8,345,299.63
    40,628,898.08
    31,374,670.07

    A. 88,646,647.81 B. 88,646,747.91
    C. 88,648,647.91 D. 88,648,747.81

32. 6,824,829.40
    682,482.94
    5,542,015.27
    775,678.51
    7,732,507.25

    A. 21,557,513.37 B. 21,567,513.37
    C. 22,567,503.37 D. 22,567,513.37

33. 22,109,405.58
    6,097,093.43
    5,050,073.99
    8,118,050.05
    4,313,980.82

    A. 45,688,593.87 B. 45,688,603.87
    C. 45,689,593.87 D. 45,689,603.87

34. 79,324,114.19
    99,848,129.74
    43,331,653.31
    41,610,207.14

    A. 264,114,104.38 B. 264,114,114.38
    C. 265,114,114.38 D. 265,214,104.38

35. 33,729,653.94
     5,959,342.58
    26,052,715.47
     4,452,669.52
     7,079,953.59

    A. 76,374,334.10   B. 76,375,334.10
    C. 77,274,335.10   D. 77,275,335.10

Questions 36-40.

DIRECTIONS: Each of Questions 36 through 40 consists of a single number in Column I and four options in Column II. For each question, you are to choose the option (A, B, C, or D) in Column II which EXACTLY matches the number in Column I.

SAMPLE QUESTION

Column I   Column II
5965121   A. 5956121
                  B. 5965121
                  C. 5966121
                  D. 5965211

The correct answer is B. Only Option B shows the number EXACTLY as it appears in Column I. Now answer Questions 36 through 40 in the same manner.

Column I   Column II
36. 9643242   A. 9643242
                           B. 9462342
                           C. 9642442
                           D. 9463242

37. 3572477   A. 3752477
                           B. 3725477
                           C. 3572477
                           D. 3574277

38. 5276101   A. 5267101
                           B. 5726011
                           C. 5271601
                           D. 5276101

39. 4469329   A. 4496329
                           B. 4469329
                           C. 4496239
                           D. 4469239

8 (#1)

40. 2326308   A. 2236308   40._____
                B. 2233608
                C. 2326308
                D. 2323608

KEY (CORRECT ANSWERS)

1.	D	11.	B	21.	A	31.	D
2.	A	12.	D	22.	C	32.	A
3.	B	13.	A	23.	B	33.	B
4.	D	14.	A	24.	D	34.	A
5.	B	15.	D	25.	A	35.	C
6.	C	16.	D	26.	B	36.	A
7.	A	17.	C	27.	D	37.	C
8.	C	18.	A	28.	A	38.	D
9.	A	19.	D	29.	C	39.	B
10.	B	20.	B	30.	C	40.	C

TEST 2

DIRECTIONS: Each question or incomplete statement is followed by several suggested answers or completions. Select the one that BEST answers the question or completes the statement. *PRINT THE LETTER OF THE CORRECT ANSWER IN THE SPACE AT THE RIGHT.*

Questions 1-5.

DIRECTIONS: Each of Questions 1 through 5 consists of a name and a dollar amount. In each question, the name and dollar amount in Column II should be an EXACT copy of the name and dollar amount in Column I. If there is:
    a mistake only in the name, mark your answer A;
    a mistake only in the dollar amount, mark your answer B;
    a mistake in both the name and the dollar amount, mark your answer C;
    no mistake in either the name or the dollar amount, mark your answer D.

SAMPLE QUESTION

Column I
George Peterson
$125.50

Column II
George Petersson
$125.50

Compare the name and dollar amount in Column II with the name and dollar amount in Column I. The name *Petersson* in Column II is spelled *Peterson* in Column I. The amount is the same in both columns. Since there is a mistake only in the name, the answer to the sample question is A. Now answer Questions 1 through 5 in the same manner.

	Column I	Column II	
1.	Susanne Shultz $3440	Susanne Schultz $3440	1.____
2.	Anibal P. Contrucci $2121.61	Anibel P. Contrucci $2112.61	2.____
3.	Eugenio Mendoza $12.45	Eugenio Mendozza $12.45	3.____
4.	Maurice Gluckstadt $4297	Maurice Gluckstadt $4297	4.____
5.	John Pampellonne $4656.94	John Pammpellonne $4566.94	5.____

53

Questions 6-11.

DIRECTIONS: Each of Questions 6 through 11 consist of a set of names and addresses, which you are to compare. In each question, the name and addresses in Column II should be an EXACT copy of the name and address in Column I. If there is:
    a mistake only in the name, mark your answer A;
    a mistake only in the address, mark your answer B;
    a mistake in both the name and address, mark your answer C;
    no mistake in either the name or address, mark your answer D.

SAMPLE QUESTION

Column I	Column II
Michael Filbert	Michael Filbert
456 Reade Street	645 Reade Street
New York, N.Y. 10013	New York, N.Y. 10013

Since there is a mistake only in the address (the street number should be 456 instead of 645), the answer to the sample question is B. Now answer Questions 6 through 11 in the same manner.

	Column I	Column II	
6.	Hilda Goettelmann 55 Lenox Rd. Brooklyn, N.Y. 11226	Hilda Goettelman 55 Lenox Ave. Brooklyn, N.Y. 11226	6.____
7.	Arthur Sherman 2522 Batchelder St. Brooklyn, N.Y. 11235	Arthur Sharman 2522 Batcheder St. Brooklyn, N.Y. 11253	7.____
8.	Ralph Barnett 300 West 28 Street New York, New York 10001	Ralph Barnett 300 West 28 Street New York, New York 10001	8.____
9.	George Goodwin 135 Palmer Avenue Staten Island, New York 10302	George Godwin 135 Palmer Avenue Staten Island, New York 10302	9.____
10.	Alonso Ramirez 232 West 79 Street New York, N.Y. 10024	Alonso Ramirez 223 West 79 Street New York, N.Y. 10024	10.____
11.	Cynthia Graham 149-34 83 Street Howard Beach, N.Y. 11414	Cynthia Graham 149-35 83 Street Howard Beach, N.Y. 11414	11.____

3 (#2)

Questions 12-20.

DIRECTIONS: Questions 12 through 20 are problems in subtraction. For each question do the subtraction and select your answer from the four choices given.

12. 232,921.85
    -179,587.68

    A. 52,433.17   B. 52,434.17
    C. 53,334.17   D. 53,343,17

    12._____

13. 5,531,876.29
    -3,897,158.36

    A. 1,634,717.93   B. 1,644,718.93
    C. 1,734,717.93   D. 1,7234,718.93

    13._____

14. 1,482,658.22
    -937,925.76

    A. 544,633.46   B. 544,732.46
    C. 545,632.46   D. 545,732.46

    14._____

15. 937,828.17
    -259,673.88

    A. 678,154.29   B. 679,154.29
    C. 688,155.39   D. 699,155.39

    15._____

16. 760,412.38
    -263,465.95

    A. 496,046.43   B. 496,946.43
    C. 496,956.43   D. 497,046.43

    16._____

17. 3,203,902.26
    -2,933,087.96

    A. 260,814.30   B. 269,824.30
    C. 270,814.30   D. 270,824.30

    17._____

18. 1,023,468.71
    -934,678.88

    A. 88,780.83   B. 88,789.83
    C. 88,880.83   D. 88,889.83

    18._____

4 (#2)

19. 831,549.47
    -772,814.78

    A. 58,734.69 B. 58,834.69
    C. 59,735.69 D. 59,834.69

19.____

20. 6,306,181.74
    -3,617,376.99

    A. 2,687,904.99 B. 2,688,904.99
    C. 2,689,804.99 D. 2,799,905.99

20.____

Questions 21-30.

DIRECTIONS: Each of Questions 21 through 30 consists of three lines of code letters and three lines of numbers. The numbers on each line should correspond with the code letters on the same line in accordance with the table below.

Code Letter	J	U	B	T	Y	D	K	R	L	P
Corresponding Number	0	1	2	3	4	5	5	7	8	9

On some of the lines, an error exists in the coding. Compare the letters and numbers in each question carefully. If you find an error or errors on:
  only *one* of the lines in the question, mark your answer A;
  any *two* lines in the question, mark your answer B;
  all *three* lines in the question, mark your answer C;
  none of the lines in the question, mark your answer D.

SAMPLE QUESTION

  BJRPYUR   2079417
  DTBPYKJ   5328460
  YKLDBLT   4685283

In the above sample, the first line is correct since each code letter listed has the correct corresponding number. On the second line, an error exists because code letter P should have the number 9 instead of the number 8. The third line is correct since each code letter listed has the correct corresponding number. Since there is an error in *one* of the three lines, the correct answer is A. Now answer Questions 21 through 30 in the same manner.

21. BYPDTJL   2495308
    PLRDTJU   9815301
    DTJRYLK   5207486

21.____

22. RPBYRJK   7934706
    PKTYLBU   9624821
    KDLPJYR   6489047

22.____

23.	TPYBUJR	3942107	23._____
	BYRKPTU	2476931	
	DUKPYDL	5169458	
24.	KBYDLPL	6345898	24._____
	BLRKBRU	2876261	
	JTULDYB	0318542	
25.	LDPYDKR	8594567	25._____
	BDKDRJL	2565708	
	BDRPLUJ	2679810	
26.	PLRLBPU	9858291	26._____
	LPYKRDJ	88936750	
	TDKPDTR	3569527	
27.	RKURPBY	7617924	27._____
	RYUKPTJ	7426930	
	RTKPTJD	7369305	
28.	DYKPBJT	5469203	28._____
	KLPJBTL	6890238	
	TKPLBJP	3698209	
29.	BTPRJYL	2397148	29._____
	LDKUTYR	8561347	
	YDBLRPJ	4528190	
30.	ULPBKYT	1892643	30._____
	KPDTRBJ	6953720	
	YLKJPTB	4860932	

KEY (CORRECT ANSWERS)

1.	A	11.	D	21.	B
2.	C	12.	C	22.	C
3.	A	13.	A	23.	D
4.	D	14.	B	24.	B
5.	C	15.	A	25.	A
6.	C	16.	B	26.	C
7.	C	17.	C	27.	A
8.	D	18.	B	28.	D
9.	A	19.	A	29.	B
10.	B	20.	B	30.	D

BASIC FUNDAMENTALS OF FILING SCIENCE

TABLE OF CONTENTS

	Page
I. COMMENTARY	1
II. BASICS OF FILING	1
1. Types of Files	1
a. Shannon File	1
b. Spindle File	1
c. Box File	1
d. Flat File	1
e. Bellows File	1
f. Vertical File	1
g. Clip File	1
h. Visible File	2
i. Rotary File	2
2. Aids in Filing	2
3. Variations of Filing Systems	2
4. Centralized Filing	2
5. Methods of Filing	3
a. Alphabetic Filing	3
b. Subject Filing	3
c. Geographical Filing	3
d. Chronological Filing	3
e. Numerical Filing	3
6. Indexing	3
7. Alphabetizing	4
III. RULES FOR INDEXING AND ALPHABETIZING	4
IV. OFFICIAL EXAMINATION DIRECTIONS AND RULES	8
1. Official Directions	8
2. Official Rules For Alphabetical Filing	9
a. Names of Individuals	9
b. Names of Business Organizations	9
3. Sample Question	9

BASIC FUNDAMENTALS OF FILING SCIENCE

I. COMMENTARY

Filing is the systematic arrangement and storage of papers, cards, forms, catalogues, etc. so that they may be found easily and quickly. The importance of an efficient filing system cannot be emphasized too strongly. The filed materials form records which may be needed quickly to settle questions that may cause embarrassing situations if such evidence is not available. In addition to keeping papers in order so that they are readily available, the filing system must also be designed to keep papers in good condition. A filing system must be planned so that papers may be filed easily, withdrawn easily, and as quickly returned to their proper place. The cost of a filing system is also an important factor

The need for a filing system arose when the businessman began to carry on negotiations on a large scale. He could no longer be intimate with the details of his business. What was needed in the early era was a spindle or pigeon-hole desk. Filing in pigeon-hole desks is now almost completely extinct. It was an unsatisfactory practice since pigeon holes were not labeled, and the desk was an untidy mess.

II. BASIS OF FILING

The science of filing is an exact one and entails a thorough understanding of basic facts, materials, and methods. An overview of this important information now follows.

1. Types of Files

    a. Shannon File: This consists of a board, at one end of which are fastened two arches which may be opened laterally.

    b. Spindle File: This consists of a metal or wood base to which is attached a long, pointed spike. Papers are pushed down on the spike as received. This file is useful for temporary retention of papers.

    c. Box File: This is a heavy cardboard or metal box, opening from the side like a book.

    d. Flat File: This consists of a series of shallow drawers or trays, arranged like drawers in a cabinet.

    e. Bellows File: This is a heavy cardboard container with alphabetized or compartment sections, the ends of which are enclosed in such a manner that they resemble an accordion.

    f. Vertical File: This consists of one or more drawers in which the papers are stood on edge, usually in folders, and are indexed by guides. A series of two or more drawers in one unit is the usual file cabinet.

    g. Clip File: This file has a large clip attached to a board and is very similar to the Shannon File.

h. Visible File: Cards are filed flat in an overlapping arrangement which leaves a part of each card visible at all times.

i. Rotary File: The rotary file has a number of visible card files attached to a post around which they can be revolved. The wheel file has visible cards which rotate around a horizontal axis.

j. Tickler File: This consists of cards or folders marked with the days of the month, in which materials are filed and turned up on the appropriate day of the month.

2. Aids in Filing

   a. Guides: Guides are heavy cardboard, pasteboard, or Bristol-board sheets the same size as folders. At the top is a tab on which is marked or printed the distinguishing letter, words, or numbers indicating the material filed in a section of the drawer.

   b. Sorting Trays: Sorting trays are equipped with alphabetical guides to facilitate the sorting of papers preparatory to placing them in a file.

   c. Coding: Once the classification or indexing caption has been determined, it must be indicated on the letter for filing purposes.

   d. Cross-Reference: Some letters or papers might easily be called for under two or more captions. For this purpose, a cross-reference card or sheet is placed in the folder or in the index.

3. Variations of Filing Systems

   a. Variadex Alphabetic Index: Provides for more effective expansion of the alphabetic system.

   b. Triple-Check Numeric Filing: Entails a multiple cross-reference, as the name implies.

   c. Variadex Filing: Makes use of color as an aid in filing.

   d. Dewey Decimal System: The system is a numeric one used in libraries or for filing library materials in an office. This special type of filing system is used where material is grouped in finely divided categories, such as in libraries. With this method, all material to be filed is divided into ten major groups, from 000 to 900, and then subdivided into tens, units, and decimals.

4. Centralized Filing

Centralized filing means keeping the files in one specific or central location. Decentralized filing means putting away papers in files of individual departments. The first step in the organization of a central filing department is to make a careful canvass of all desks in the offices. In this manner we can determine just what material needs to be filed, and what information each desk occupant requires from the central file. Only papers which may be used at some time by persons in the various offices should be placed in the central file. A paper that is to be used at some time by persons in the various offices should be placed in the central file. A paper that is to be used by one department only should never be filed in the central file.

5. Methods of Filing

While there are various methods used for filing, actually there are only five basic systems: alphabetical, subject, numerical, geographic, and chronological. All other systems are derived from one of these or from a combination of two or more of them. Since the purpose of a filing system is to store business records systemically so that any particular record can be found almost instantly when required, filing requires, in addition to the proper kinds of equipment and supplies, an effective method of indexing.
There are five basic systems of filing:

a. Alphabetic Filing: Most filing is alphabetical. Other methods, as described below, require extensive alphabetization. In alphabetical filing, lettered dividers or guides are arranged in alphabetic sequence. Material to be filed is placed behind the proper guide. All materials under each letter are also arranged alphabetically. Folders are used unless the file is a card index.

b. Subject Filing: This method is used when a single, complete file on a certain subject is desired. A subject file is often maintained to assemble all correspondence on a certain subject. Such files are valuable in connection with insurance claims, contract negotiations, personnel, and other investigations, special programs, and similar subjects.

c. Geographical File: Materials are filed according to location: states, cities, counties, or other subdivisions. Statistics and tax information are often filed in this manner.

d. Chronological File: Records are filed according to date. This method is used especially in "tickler" files that have guides numbered 1 to 31 for each day of the month. Each number indicates the day of the month when the filed item requires attention.

e. Numerical File: This method requires an alphabetic card index giving name and number. The card index is used to locate records numbered consecutively in the files according to date received or sequence in which issued, such as licenses, permits, etc.

6. Indexing

Determining the name or title under which an item is to be filed is known as indexing. For example, how would a letter from Robert E. Smith be filed? The name would be rearranged Smith, Robert E., so that the letter would be filed under the last name.

7. Alphabetizing

The arranging of names for filing is known as alphabetizing. For example, suppose you have four letters indexed under the names Johnson, Becker, Roe, and Stern. How should these letters be arranged in the files so that they may be found easily? You would arrange the four names alphabetically, thus Becker, Johnson, Roe, and Stern.

III. RULES FOR INDEXING AND ALPHABETIZING

1. The names of persons are to be transposed. Write the surname first, then the given name, and, finally, the middle name or initial. Then arrange the various names according to the alphabetic order of letters throughout the entire name. If there is a title, consider that after the middle name or initial.

NAMES	INDEXED AS
Arthur L. Bright	Bright, Arthur L.
Arthur S. Bright	Bright, Arthur S.
P.E. Cole	Cole, P.E.
Dr. John C. Fox	Fox, John C. (Dr.)

2. If a surname includes the same letters of another surname, with one or more additional letters added to the end, the shorter surname is placed first regardless of the given name or the initial of the given name.

NAMES	INDEXED AS
Robert E. Brown	Brown, Robert E.
Gerald A. Browne	Browne, Gerald A.
William O. Brownell	Brownell, William O.

3. Firm names are alphabetized under the surnames. Words like the, an, a, of, and for, are not considered.

NAMES	INDEXED AS
Bank of America	Bank of America
Bank Discount Dept.	Bank Discount Dept.
The Cranford Press	Cranford Press, The
Nelson Dwyer & Co.	Dwyer, Nelson, & Co.
Sears, Roebuck & Co.	Sears Roebuck & Co.
Montgomery Ward & Co.	Ward, Montgomery, & Co.

4. The order of filing is determined first of all by the first letter of the names to be filed. If the first letters are the same, the order is determined by the second letters, and so on. In the following pairs of names, the order is determined by the letters underlined:

    | Austen | Hayes | Hanson | Harvey | Heath | Green | Schwartz |
    | Baker | Heath | Harper | Harwood | Heaton | Greene | Schwarz |

5. When surnames are alike, those with initials only precede those with given names, unless the first initial comes alphabetically after the first letter of the name.

    Gleason, S.   *but,* Abbott, Mary
    Gleason, S.W.   Abbott, W.B.
    Gleason, Sidney

6. Hyphenated names are treated as if spelled without the hyphen.
    Lloyd, Paul N.   Lloyd, Robert
    Lloyd-Jones, James   Lloyd-Thomas, A.S.

7. Company names composed of single letters which are not used as abbreviations precede the other names beginning with the same letter.
    B & S Garage   E Z Duplicator Co.
    B X Cable Co.   Eagle Typewriter Co.
    Babbitt, R.N.   Edison Company

8. The ampersand (&) and the apostrophe (') in firm names are disregarded in alphabetizing.
    Nelson & Niller   M & C Amusement Corp.
    Nelson, Walter J.   M C Art Assn.
    Nelson's Bakery

9. Names beginning with Mac, Mc, or M' are usually placed in regular order as spelled. Some filing systems file separately names beginning with Mc.
    MacDonald, R.J.   Mazza, Anthony
    MacDonald, S.B.   McAdam, Wm.
    Mace, Wm.   McAndrews, Jerry

10. Names beginning with St. are listed as if the name Saint were spelled in full. Numbered street names and all abbreviated names are treated as if spelled out in full.
    Saginaw   Fifth Avenue Hotel   Hart Mfg. Co.
    St. Louis   42nd Street Dress Shop   Hart, Martin
    St. Peter's Rectory Hart, Chas.   Hart, Thos.
    Sandford   Hart, Charlotte   Hart, Thomas A.
    Smith, Wm.   Hart, Jas.   Hart, Thos. R.
    Smith, Willis   Hart, Janice

11. Federal, state, or city departments of government should be placed alphabetically under the governmental branch controlling them.
    Illinois, State of – Departments and Commissions
        Banking Dept.
        Employment Bureau
    United States Government Departments
        Commerce
        Defense
        State
        Treasury

12. Alphabetic Order: Each word in a name is an indexing unit. Arrange the names in alphabetic order by comparing similar units in each name. Consider the second units only when the first units are identical. Consider the third units only when both the first and second units are identical.

13. Single Surnames or Initials: A surname, when used alone, precedes the same surname with a first name or initial. A surname with a first initial only precedes a surname with a complete first name. This rule is sometimes stated, "nothing comes before something."

14. Surname Prefixes: A surname prefix is not a separate indexing unit, but it is considered part of the surname. These prefixes include: d', D', Da, de, De, Del, Des, Di, Du, Fitz., La, Le, Mc, Mac, 'c, O', St., Van, Van der, Von, Von der, and others. The prefixes M', Mac, and Mc are indexed and filed exactly as they are spelled.

15. Names of Firms: Names of firms and institutions are indexed and filed exactly as they are written when they do not contain the complete name of an individual.

16. Names of Firms Containing Complete Individual Names: When the firm or institution name includes the complete name of an individual, the units are transposed for indexing in the same way as the name of an individual.

17. Article "The": When the article "the" occurs at the beginning of a name, it is placed at the end in parentheses but it is not moved. In both cases, it is not an indexing unit and is disregarded in filing.

18. Hyphenated Names: Hyphenated firm names are considered as separate indexing units. Hyphenated surnames of individuals are considered as one indexing unit; this applies also to hyphenated names of individuals whose complete names are part of a firm name.

19. Abbreviations: Abbreviations are considered as though the name were written in full; however, single letters other than abbreviations are considered as separate indexing units.

20. Conjunctions, Prepositions, and Firm Endings: Conjunctions and prepositions, such as and, for, in, of, are disregarded in indexing and filing but are not omitted or their order changed when writing names on cards and folders. Firm endings, such as Ltd., Inc., So., Son, Bros., Mfg., and Corp. , are treated as a unit in indexing and filing and are considered as though spelled in full, such as Brothers and Incorporated.

21. One of Two Words: Names that may be spelled either as one or two words are indexed and filed as one word.

22. Compound Geographic Names: Compound geographic names are considered as separate indexing and filing units, except when the first part of the name is not an English word, such as the Los in Los Angeles.

23. Titles or degrees of individuals, whether preceding or following the name, are not considered in indexing or filing. They are placed in parentheses after the given name or initial. Terms that designate seniority, such as Jr., Sr., 2d, are also placed in parentheses and are considered for indexing and filing only when the names to be indexed are otherwise identical.

Exception A: When the name of an individual consists of a title and one name only, such as Queen Elizabeth, it is not transposed and the title is considered for indexing and filing.

Exception B: When a title or foreign article is the initial word of a firm or association name, it is considered for indexing and filing.

24. Possessives: When a word ends in apostrophe s, the s is not considered in indexing and filing. However, when a word ends in s apostrophe, because the s is part of the original word, it is considered. This rule is sometimes stated, "Consider everything up to the apostrophe."

25. United States and Foreign Government Names: Names pertaining to the federal government are indexed and filed under United States Government and then subdivided by title of the department, bureau, division, commission, or board. Names pertaining to foreign governments are indexed and filed under names of countries and then subdivided by title of the department, bureau, division, commission, or board. Phrases, such as department of, bureau of, division of, commission of, board of, when used in titles of governmental bodies, are placed in parentheses after the word they modify, but are disregarded in indexing and filing. Such phrases, however, are considered in indexing and filing governmental names.

26. Other Political Subdivisions: Names pertaining to other political subdivisions, such as states, counties, cities, or towns, are indexed and filed under the name of the political subdivision and then subdivided by the title of the department, bureau, division, commission, or board.

27. When the same name appears with different addresses, the names are indexed as usual and arranged alphabetically according to city or town. The State is considered only when there is duplication of both individual or company name and city name. If the same name is located at different addresses within the same city, then the names are arranged alphabetically by streets. If the same name is located at more than one address on the same street then the names are arranged from the lower to the higher street number.

28. Numbers: Any number in a name is considered as though it were written in words, and it is indexed and filed as one unit.

29. Bank Names: Because the names of many banking institutions are alike in several respects, as First National Bank, Second National Bank, etc., banks are indexed and filed first by city location, then by bank name, with the state location written in parentheses and considered only if necessary.

30. Married Women: The legal name of a married woman is the one used for filing purposes. Legally, a man's surname is the only part of a man's name a woman assumes when she marries. Her legal name, therefore, could be either:
    a. Her own first and middle names together with her husband's surname, or
    b. Her own first name and maiden surname, together with her husband's surname.

Mrs. is placed in parentheses at the end of the name. Her husband's first and middle names are given in parentheses below her legal name.

31. An alphabetically arranged list of names illustrating many difficult points of alphabetizing follows:

COLUMN I	COLUMN II
Abbot, W.B.	54th St. Tailor Shop
Abbot, Alice	Forstall, W.J.
Allen Alexander B.	44th St. Garage
Allen, Alexander B., Inc.	M A Delivery Co.
Andersen, Hans	M & C Amusement Corp.
Andersen, Hans E.	M C Art Assn.
Andersen, Hans E., Jr.	MacAdam, Wm.
Anderson, Andrew Andrews,	Macaulay, James
George Brown Motor Co., Boston	MacAulay, Wilson
Brown Motor Co., Chicago	MacDonald, R.J.
Brown Motor Co., Philadelphia	Macdonald, S. B.
Brown Motor Co., San Francisco	Mace, Wm.
Dean, Anna	Mazza, Anthony
Dean, Anna F.	McAdam, Wm.
Dean, Anna Frances	McAndrews, Jerry
Dean & Co.	Meade & Clark Co.
Deane-Arnold Apartments	Meade, S.T.
Deane's Pharmacy	Meade, Soloman
Deans, Felix A.	Sackett Publishing Co.
Dean's Studio	Sacks, Robert
Deans, Wm.	St. Andrew Hotel
Deans & Williams	St. John, Homer W.
East Randolph	Saks, Isaac B.
East St. Louis	Stephens, Ira
Easton, Pa.	Stevens, Delevan
Eastport, Me.	Stevens, Delila

IV. OFFICIAL EXAMINATION DIRECTIONS AND RULES

To preclude the possibility of conflicting or varying methods of filing, explicit directions and express rules are given to the candidate before he answers the filing questions on an examination.
The most recent official directions and rules for the filing questions are given immediately hereafter.

OFFICIAL DIRECTIONS

Each of questions...to...consists of four (five) names. For each question, select the one of the four(five) names that should be first (second)(third)(last) if the four (five(names were arranged in alphabetical order in accordance with the rules for alphabetical filing given below. Read these rules carefully. Then, for each question, indicate in the correspondingly numbered row on the answer sheet the letter preceding the name that should be first(second)(third)(last) in alphabetical order.

OFFICIAL RULES FOR ALPHABETICAL FILING

Names of Individuals

1. The names of individuals are filed in strict alphabetical order, first according to the last name, then according to first name or initial, and, finally, according to middle name or initial. For example: William Jones precedes George Kirk and Arthur S. Blake precedes Charles M. Blake.
2. When the last names are identical, the one with an initial instead of a first name precedes the one "with a first name beginning with the same initial." For example: J. Green precedes Joseph Green.
3. When identical last names also have identical first names, the one without a middle name or initial precedes the one with a middle name or initial. For example: Robert Jackson precedes both Robert C. Jackson and Robert Chester Jackson.
4. When last names are identical and the first names are also identical, the one with a middle initial precedes the one with a middle name beginning with the same initial. For example: Peter A. Brown precedes Peter Alvin Brown.
5. Prefixes such as De, El, La, and Van are considered parts of the names they precede. For example: Wilfred DeWald precedes Alexander Duval.
6. Last names beginning with "Mac" or "Mc" are filed as spelled.
7. Abbreviated names are treated as if they were spelled out. For example: Jos. is filed as Joseph and Robt. is filed as Robert.
8. Titles and designations such as Dr., Mrs., Prof. are disregarding in filing.

Names of Business Organizations

1. The names of business organizations are filed exactly as written, except that an organization bearing the name of an individual is filed alphabetically according to the name of the individual in accordance with the rules for filing names of individuals given above. For example: Thomas Allison Machine Company precedes Northern Baking Company.
2. When numerals occur in a name, they are treated as if they were spelled out. For example: 6 stands for six and 4th stands for fourth.
3. When the following words occur in names, they are disregarded: the, of

SAMPLE QUESTION

Choose the name that should be filed third.
A. Fred Town (2)   B. Jack Towne (3)   C. D. Town (1)   D. Jack Stone (4)
The numbers in parentheses indicate the proper alphabetical order in which these names should be filed. Since the name that should be filed third is Jack Towne, the answer is (B).

FILING

EXAMINATION SECTION

TEST 1

DIRECTIONS: Each of the following questions contains four names. For each question, choose the name that should be FIRST if the four names are to be arranged in alphabetical order in accordance with the Rules for Alphabetical Filing given before. Read these rules carefully. Then, for each question, indicate in the space at the right the letter before the name that should be FIRST in alphabetical order.

SAMPLE QUESTION
A. Jane Earl   (2)
B. James A. Earle (4)
C. James Earl   (1)
D. J. Earle   (3)

The numbers in parentheses show the proper alphabetical order in which these names should be filed. Since the name that should be filed FIRST is James Earl, the answer to the Sample Question is C.

1. A. Majorca Leather Goods   B. Robert Maiorca and Sons   1.____
    C. Maintenance Management Corp.   D. Majestic Carpet Mills

2. A. Municipal Telephone Service   B. Municipal Reference Library   2.____
    C. Municipal Credit Union   D. Municipal Broadcasting System

3. A. Robert B. Pierce   B. R. Bruce Pierce   3.____
    C. Ronald Pierce   D. Robert Bruce Pierce

4. A. Four Seasons Sports Club   B. 14 Street Shopping Center   4.____
    C. Forty Thieves Restaurant   D. 42nd St. Theaters

5. A. Franco Franceschini   B. Amos Franchini   5.____
    C. Sandra Franceschia   D. Lilie Franchinesca

KEY (CORRECT ANSWERS)

1. C
2. D
3. B
4. D
5. C

TEST 2

DIRECTIONS: Each of the following questions contains four names. For each question, choose the name that should be FIRST if the four names are to be arranged in alphabetical order in accordance with the Rules for Alphabetical Filing given before. Read these rules carefully. Then, for each question, indicate in the space at the right the letter before the name that should be FIRST in alphabetical order.

    SAMPLE QUESTION
    A. Jane Earl   (2)
    B. James A. Earle   (4)
    C. James Earl   (1)
    D. J. Earle   (3)

The numbers in parentheses show the proper alphabetical order in which these names should be filed. Since the name that should be filed FIRST is James Earl, the answer to the Sample Question is C.

1. A. Alan Carson, M.D.   B. The Andrew Carlton Nursing Home
   C. Prof., Alfred P. Carlton   D. Mr. A. Peter Carlton

2. A. Chas. A. Denner   B. H. Jeffrey Dener
   C. Charles Denner   D. Harold Dener

3. A. James C. Maziola   B. Joseph A. Mazzola
   C. James Maziola   D. J. Alfred Mazzola

4. A. Bureau of Family Affairs   B. Office of the Comptroller
   C. Department of Gas & Electricity   D. Board of Estimate

5. A. Robert Alan Pearson   B. John Charles Pierson
   C. Robert Allen Pearson   D. John Chester Pierson

6. A. The Johnson Manufacturing Co.   B. C.J. Johnston
   C. Bernard Johnsen   D. Prof. Corey Johnstone

7. A. Ninteenth Century Book Shop   B. Ninth Federal Bank
   C. 19th Hole Coffee Shop   D. 92nd St. Station

8. A. George S. McNeely   B. Hugh J. Macintosh
   C. Mr. G. Stephen McNeally   D. Mr. H. James Macintosh

KEY (CORRECT ANSWERS)

1. D
2. B
3. C
4. B
5. A
6. C
7. A
8. D

TEST 3

DIRECTIONS: Each of the following questions contains four names. For each question, choose the name that should be LAST if the four names are to be arranged in alphabetical order in accordance with the Rules for Alphabetical Filing given before. Read these rules carefully. Then, for each question, indicate in the space at the right the letter before the name that should be LAST in alphabetical order.

SAMPLE QUESTION
A. Jane Earl   (2)
B. James A. Earle (4)
C. James Earl   (1)
D. J. Earle   (3)

The numbers in parentheses show the proper alphabetical order in which these names should be filed. Since the name that should be filed LAST is James A. Earle, the answer to the Sample Question is B.

1. A. Steiner, Michael   B. Steinblau, Dr. Walter   1.____
    C. Steinet, Gary   D. Stein, Prof. Edward

2. A. The Paper Goods Warehouse B. T. Pane and Sons Inc.   2.____
    C. Paley, Wallace   D. Painting Supplies Inc.

3. A. D'Angelo, F.   B. De Nove, C.   3.____
    C. Daniels, Frank   D. Dovarre, Carl

4. A. Berene, Arnold   B. Berene, Arnold L.   4.____
    C. Beren, Arnold Lee   D. Berene, A.

5. A. Kallinski, Liza   B. Kalinsky, L.   5.____
    C. Kallinky, E.   D. Kallinsky, Elizabeth

6. A. Morgenom, Salvatore   B. Megan, J.   6.____
    C. J. Morgenthal Consultant Services D. Morgan, Janet

7. A. Ritter, G.   B. Ritter, George   7.____
    B. Riter, George H.   D. Ritter, G.H.

8. A. Wheeler, Adele N.   B. Wieler, Ada   8.____
    C. Weiler, Adelaide   D. Wheiler, Adele

9. A. Macan, Toby   B. Maccini, T.   9.____
    C. MacAvoy, Thomas   D. Mackel, Theodore

10. A. Loomus, Kenneth   B. Lomis Paper Supplies   10.____
    C. Loo, N.   D. Loomis Machine Repair Company

KEY (CORRECT ANSWERS)

1. C
2. A
3. D
4. B
5. D
6. C
7. B
8. B
9. D
10. A

TEST 4

DIRECTIONS: In the following questions there are five notations numbered 1 through 5 shown in Column I. Each notation is made up of a supplier's name, a contract number, and a date and is to be filed according to the following rules:

First: File in alphabetical order
Second: When two or more notations have the same supplier, file according to the contract number in numerical order beginning with the lowest number.
Third: When two or more notations have the same supplier and contract number, file according to the date beginning with the earliest date.

In Column II the numbers 1 through 5 are arranged in four ways to show different possible orders in which the merchandise information might be filed. Pick the answer (A, B, C, or D) in Column II in which the notations are arranged according to the above filing rules.

SAMPLE QUESTION

COLUMN I
1. Cluney   (4865)   6/17/72
2. Roster   (2466)   5/10/71
3. Altool   (7114)   10/15/72
4. Cluney   (5276)   12/18/71
5. Cluney   (4865)   4/8/72

COLUMN II
A. 2, 3, 4, 1, 5
B. 2, 5, 1, 3, 4
C. 3, 2, 1, 4, 5
D. 3, 5, 1, 4, 2

The correct way to file the notations is:
3. Altool   (7114)   10/15/72
5. Cluney   (4865)   4/8/72
1. Cluney   (4865)   6/17/72
4. Cluney   (5276)   12/18/71
2. Roster   (2466)   5/10/71

The correct filing order is shown by the numbers in front of each name (3, 5, 1, 4, 2). The answer to the Sample Question is the letter in Column II in front of the numbers 3, 5, 1, 4, 2. This answer is D.

COLUMN I
1. 1. Fenten   (38511)   1/4/73
   2. Meadowlane (5020)   11/1/72
   3. Whitehall   (36142)   6/22/72
   4. Clinton   (4141)   5/26/71
   5. Mester   (8006)   4/20/71

COLUMN II
A. 3, 5, 2, 1, 4
B. 4, 1, 2, 5, 3
C. 4, 2, 5, 3, 1
D. 5, 4, 3, 1, 2

1.____

2. 1. Harvard   (2286)   2/19/70
   2. Parker   (1781)   4/12/71
   3. Lenson   (9044)   6/6/72
   4. Brothers   (38380)   10/11/72
   5. Parker   (41400)   12/20/70

A. 2, 4, 3, 1, 5
B. 2, 1, 3, 4, 5
C. 4, 1, 3, 2, 5
D. 5, 2, 3, 1, 4

2.____

2 (#4)

		COLUMN I			COLUMN II	
3.	1.	Newtone	(3197)	8/22/70	A. 1, 4, 2, 5, 3	3.____
	2.	Merritt	(4071)	8/8/72	B. 4, 2, 1, 5, 3	
	3.	Writebest	(60666)	4/7/71	C. 4, 5, 2, 1, 3	
	4.	Maltons	(34380)	3/30/72	D. 5, 2, 4, 3, 1	
	5.	Merrit	(4071)	7/16/71		
4.	1.	Weinburt	(45514)	6/4/71	A. 4, 5, 2, 1, 3	4.____
	2.	Owntye	(35860)	10/3/71	B. 4,2, 5, 3, 1	
	3.	Weinburt	(45514)	2/1/71	C. 4, 2, 5, 1, 3	
	4.	Fasttex	(7677)	11/10/71	D. 4, 5, 2, 3, 1	
	5.	Owntye	(4574)	7/17/71		
5.	1.	Premier	(1003)	7/29/70	A. 2, 1, 4, 3, 5	5.____
	2.	Phylson	(0031)	5/5/71	B. 3, 5, 4, 1, 2	
	3.	Lathen	(3328)	10/3/71	C. 4, 1, 2, 3, 5	
	4.	Harper	(8046)	8/18/72	D. 4, 3, 5, 2, 1	
	5.	Lathen	(3328)	12/1/72		
6.	1.	Repper	(46071)	10/14/72	A. 3, 2, 4, 5, 1	6.____
	2.	Destex	(77271)	8/27/72	B. 3, 4, 2, 5, 1	
	3.	Clawson	(30736)	7/28/71	C. 3, 4, 5, 2, 1	
	4.	Destex	(77271)	8/17/71	D. 3, 5, 4, 2, 1	
	5.	Destex	(77271)	4/14/71		

KEY (CORRECT ANSWERS)

1. B
2. C
3. C
4. A
5. D
6. C

1. C
2. A
3. B
4. D

2 (#5)

		COLUMN I			COLUMN II	

5. 1. Abernathy   (712467)   6/23/20   A. 5, 3, 1, 2, 4   5._____
    2. Acevedo   (680262)   6/23/18   B. 5, 4, 2, 3, 1
    3. Aaron   (967647)   1/17/19   C. 1, 3, 5, 2, 4
    4. Acevedo   (680622)   5/14/17   D. 2, 4, 1, 5, 3
    5. Aaron   (967647)   4/1/15

6. 1. Simon   (645219)   8/19/20   A. 4, 1, 2, 5, 3   6._____
    2. Simon   (645219)   9/2/18   B. 4, 5, 2, 1, 3
    3. Simons   (645218)   7/7/20   C. 3, 5, 2, 1, 4
    4. Simms   (646439)   10/12/21   D. 5, 1, 2, 3, 4
    5. Simon   (645219)   10/16/17

7. 1. Rappaport   (312230)   6/11/21   A. 4, 3, 1, 2, 5   7._____
    2. Rascio   (777510)   2/9/20   B. 4, 3, 1, 5, 2
    3. Rappaport   (312230)   7/3/17   C. 3, 4, 1, 5, 2
    4. Rapaport   (312330)   9/6/20   D. 5, 2, 4, 3, 1
    5. Rascio   (777501)   7/7/20

8. 1. Johnson   (843250)   6/8/17   A. 1, 3, 2, 4, 5   8._____
    2. Johnson   (843205)   4/3/20   B. 1, 3, 2, 5, 4
    3. Johnson   (843205)   8/6/17   C. 3, 2, 1, 4, 5
    4. Johnson   (843602)   3/8/21   D. 3, 2, 1, 5, 4
    5. Johnson   (843602)   8/3/20

KEY (CORRECT ANSWERS)

1. C   5. A
2. A   6. B
3. C   7. B
4. D   8. D

TEST 6

DIRECTIONS: In each of the following questions there are four groups of names. One of the groups in each question is NOT in correct alphabetic order. Mark the letter of that group next to the number that corresponds to the number of the question.

1. A. Ace Advertising Agency; Acel, Erwin; Ad Graphics; Ade, E.J. & Co.
   B. Advertising Bureau, Inc.; Advertising Guild, Inc.; Advertising Ideas, Inc.; Advertising Sales Co.
   C. Allan Associates; Allen-Wayne, Inc.; Alley & Richards, Inc.; Allum, Ralph
   D. Anderson & Cairnes; Amos Parrish & Co.; Anderson Merrill Co.; Anderson, Milton

   1.____

2. A. Bach, Henry; Badillo, John; Baer, Budd; Bair, Albert
   B. Baker, Lynn; Bakers, Albert; Bailin, Henry; Bakers Franchise Corp.
   C. Bernhardt, Manfred; Bernstein, Jerome; Best, Frank; Benton Associates
   D. Brandford, Edward; Branstatter Associates; Brown, Martel; Browne, Bert

   2.____

3. A. Cone, Robert; Contempo, Bernard; Conti Advertising; Cooper, James
   B. Cramer, Zed; Creative Sales; Crofton, Ada; Cromwell, Samuel
   C. Cheever, Fred; Chernow Advertising; Chenault Associates; Chester, Arthur
   D. Chain Store Advertising; Chair Lawrence & Co.; Chaite, Alexander E.; Chase, Luis

   3.____

4. A. Delahanty, Francis; Dela McCarthy Associates; Delehanty, Kurnit; Delroy, Stewart
   B. Doerfler, B.R.; Doherty, Clifford; Dorchester Apartments; Dorchester, Monroe
   C. Drayer, Stella; Dreher, Norton; Dreyer, Harvey; Dryer, Lester
   D. Duble, Normal; Duevell, William C.; Du Fine, August; Dugan, Harold

   4.____

5. A. Esmond, Walter; Esty, Willia; Ettinger, Carl; Everett, Austin
   B. Enlos, Cartez; Entertainment, Inc.; Englemore, Irwin; Equity Associates
   C. Einhorn, Anna Mrs.; Einhorn, Arlene; Eisele, Mary; Eisele, Minnie Mrs.
   D. Eagen, Roy; Egale, George; Egan, Barrett; Eisen, Henry

   5.____

6. A. Funt, Rand Inc.; Furman, Fainer & Co.; Furman Roth & Co.; Fusco, Frank A.
   B. Friedan, Phillip; Friedman, Mitchell; Friend, Harvey; Friend, Herbert
   C. Folkart Greeting Cards; Food Service; Foote, Cornelius; Foreign Advertising
   D. Finkels, Eliot; Finnerman, John; Finneran, Joseph; Firestone, Albert

   6.____

7. A. Gubitz, Jay; Guild, Dorothy; Gumbiner, B.; Gussow, Leonard
   B. Gore, Smith; Gotham Art, Inc.; Gotham Editors Service; Gotham-Vladimir, Inc.
   C. Georgian, Wolf; Gerdts, H.J.; German News Co.; Germaine, Werner
   D. Gardner, Fred; Gardner, Roy; Garner, Roy; Gaynor & Ducal Inc.

   7.____

2 (#6)

8. A. Howard, E. T.; Howard, Francis; Howson, Allen; Hoyt, Charles
   B. Houston, Byron; House of Graphics; Rowland, Lynne; Hoyle, Mortimer
   C. Hi-Lite Art Service; Hickerson, J.M.; Hickey, Murphy; Hicks; Gilbert
   D. Hyman, Bram; Hyman, Charles B.; Hyman, Claire; Hyman, Claude

8.____

9. A. Idone, Leopold; Ingraham, Evelyn; Ianuzzi, Frank; Itkin, Simon
   B. Ideas, Inc.; Inter-Racial Press, Inc.; International Association; Iverson, Ford
   C. Il Trionofo; Inwood Bake Shop; Iridor, Rose; Italian Pastry
   D. Ionadi, Anthony Irena, Louise; Iris, Ysabella; Isabelle, Arlia

9.____

10. A. Jonas, Myron; Johnstone, John; Jones, Julius; Joptha, Meyer
    B. Jeanne's Beauty Shoppe; Jeger, Jans; Jem, H.; Jim's Grill
    C. Jacobs, Abraham & Co., Jacobs, Harold A.; Jacobs, Joseph; Jacobs, M.J.
    D. Japan Air Lines; Jensen, Arne; Judson, P.; Juliano, Jeremiah

10.____

KEY (CORRECT ANSWERS)

1.	D	6.	D
2.	B	7.	C
3.	C	8.	B
4.	A	9.	A
5.	B	10.	A

TEST 7

DIRECTIONS: Below are ten groups of names, numbered 1 through 10. For each group, three different filing arrangements of the names in the group are given. In only ONE of these arrangements are the names in correct filing order according to standard rules for filing. For each group, select the ONE arrangement, lettered A, B, C, that is CORRECT.

1. Arrangement A
   Nichols, C. Arnold
   Nichols, Bruce
   Nicholson, Arthur

   Arrangement B
   Nichols, Bruce
   Nichols, C. Arnold
   Nicholson, Arthur

   Arrangement C
   Nicholson, Arthur
   Nichols, Bruce
   Nichols, C. Arnold

   1.____

2. Arrangement A
   Schaefer's Drug Store
   Schaefer, Harry T.
   Schaefer Bros.

   Arrangement B
   Schaefer Bros.
   Schaefer, Harry T.
   Schaefer's Drug Store

   Arrangement C
   Schaefer Bros.
   Schaefer's Drug Store
   Schaefer, Harry T.

   2.____

3. Arrangement A
   Adams' Dime Store
   Adami, David
   Adams, Donald

   Arrangement B
   Adami, David
   Adams' Dime Store
   Adams, Donald

   Arrangement C
   Adami, David
   Adams. Donald
   Adams' Dime Store

   3.____

4. Arrangement A
   Newton, Jas. F.
   Newton, Janet
   Newton-Jarvis Law Firm

   Arrangement B
   Newton-Jarvis Law Firm
   Newton, Jas. F.
   Newton, Janet

   Arrangement C
   Newton, Janet
   Newton-Jarvis Law Firm
   Newton, Jas. F.

   4.____

5. Arrangement A
   Radford and Bigelow
   Radford Transfer Co.
   Radford-Smith, Albert

   Arrangement B
   Radford and Bigelow
   Radford-Smith, Albert
   Radford Transfer Co.

   Arrangement C
   Radford Transfer Co.
   Radford and Bigelow
   Radford-Smith, Albert

   5.____

6. Arrangement A
   Trent, Inc.
   Trent Farm Products
   20th Century Film Corp.

   Arrangement B
   20th Century Film Corp.
   Trent Farm Products
   Trent, Inc.

   Arrangement C
   Trent Farm Products
   Trent, Inc.
   20th Century Film Corp.

   6.____

7. Arrangement A
   Morrell, Ralph
   M.R.B. Paper Co.
   Mt. Ranier Hospital

   Arrangement B
   Morrell, Ralph
   Mt. Ranier Hospital
   M.R.B. Paper Co.

   Arrangement C
   M.R.B. Paper Co.
   Morrell, Ralph
   Mt. Ranier Hospital

   7.____

8. Arrangement A
   Vanity Faire Shop
   Van Loon, Charles
   The Williams Magazine Corp.

   Arrangement B
   The Williams Magazine Corp.
   Van Loon, Charles
   Vanity Faire Shop

   Arrangement C
   Van Loon, Charles
   Vanity Faire Shop

   8.____

9.   Arrangement A   Arrangement B   Arrangement C   9.____
      Crane and Jones Ins. Co.   L.J. Coughtry Mfg. Co.   Little Folks Shop
      Little Folks Shop   Crane and Jones Ins. Co.   L.J. Coughtry Mfg. Co.
      L.J. Coughtry Mfg. Co.   Little Folks Shop   Crane and Jones Ins. Co.

10.   Arrangement A   Arrangement B   Arrangement C   10.____
      South Arlington Garage   N.Y. State Dept. of Audit   State Antique Shop
      N.Y. State Dept. of Audit   and Control   South Arlington Garage
         and Control   South Arlington Garage   N.Y. State Dept. of Audit
      State Antique Shop   State Antique Shop   and Control

KEY (CORRECT ANSWERS)

1.	B	6.	C
2.	C	7.	A
3.	B	8.	A
4.	A	9.	B
5.	B	10.	B

TEST 8

DIRECTIONS: Below are ten groups of names, numbered 1 through 10. For each group, three different filing arrangements of the names in the group are given. In only ONE of these arrangements are the names in correct filing order according to standard rules for filing. For each group, select the ONE arrangement, lettered A, B, C, that is CORRECT.

1. Arrangement A
   Gillilan, William
   Gililane, Ethel
   Gillihane, Harry

   Arrangement B
   Gililane, Ethel
   Gillihane, Harry
   Gillilan, William

   Arrangement C
   Gillihane, Harry
   Gillilan, William
   Gililane, Ethel

   1.____

2. Arrangement A
   Stevens, J. Donald
   Stevenson, David
   Stevens, James

   Arrangement B
   Stevenson, David
   Stevens, J. Donald
   Stevens, James

   Arrangement C
   Stevens, J. Donald
   Stevens, James
   Stevenson, David

   2.____

3. Arrangement A
   Brooks, Arthur E.
   Brooks, H. Albert
   Brooks, H.T.

   Arrangement B
   Brooks, H.T.
   Brooks, H. Albert
   Brooks, Arthur E.

   Arrangement C
   Brooks, H. Albert
   Brooks, Arthur E.
   Brooks, H.T.

   3.____

4. Arrangement A
   Lafayette, Earl
   Le Grange, Wm. J.
   La Roux Haberdashery

   Arrangement B
   Le Grange, Wm. J.
   La Roux Haberdashery
   Lafayette, Earl

   Arrangement C
   Lafayette, Earl
   La Roux Haberdashery
   Le Grange, Wm. J.

   4.____

5. Arrangement A
   Mosher Bros.
   Mosher's Auto Repair
   Mosher, Dorothy

   Arrangement B
   Mosher's Auto Repair
   Mosher Bros.
   Mosher, Dorothy

   Arrangement C
   Mosher Bros.
   Mosher, Dorothy
   Mosher's Auto Repair

   5.____

6. Arrangement A
   Ainsworth, Inc.
   Ainsworth, George
   Air-O-Pad Co.

   Arrangement B
   Ainsworth, George
   Ainsworth, Inc.
   Air-O-Pad Co.

   Arrangement C
   Air-O-Pad Co.
   Ainsworth, George
   Ainsworth, Inc.

   6.____

7. Arrangement A
   Peters' Printing Co.
   Peerbridge, Alfred
   Peters, Paul

   Arrangement B
   Peterbridge, Alfred
   Peters, Paul
   Petters' Printing Co.

   Arrangement C
   Peters, Paul
   Peters' Printing Co.
   Peterbridge, Alfred

   7.____

8. Arrangement A
   Sprague-Miller, Elia
   Sprague (and) Reed
   Sprague Insurance Co.

   Arrangement B
   Sprague (and) Reed
   Sprague Insurance Co.
   Sprague-Miller, Ella

   Arrangement C
   Sprague Insurance Co.
   Sprague (and) Reed
   Sprague-Miller, Ella

   8.____

9. Arrangement A
    Ellis, Chalmers Adv.
       Agency
    Ellis, Chas.
    Ellis, Charlotte

    Arrangement B
    Ellis, Chas.
    Ellis, Charlotte
    Ellis, Chalmers Adv.
       Agency

    Arrangement C
    Ellis, Charlotte
    Ellis, Chas.
    Ellis, Chalmers Adv.
       Agency

    9.____

10. Arrangement A
    Adams, Paul
    Five Acres Coffee Shop
    Fielding Adjust. Co.

    Arrangement B
    Five Acres Coffee Shop
    Adams, Paul
    Fielding Adjust. Co.

    Arrangement C
    Adams, Paul
    Fielding Adjust Co.
    Five Acres Coffee Shop

    10.____

KEY (CORRECT ANSWERS)

1.	B	6.	B
2.	C	7.	B
3.	A	8.	C
4.	C	9.	A
5.	B	10.	C

TEST 9

DIRECTIONS: Below in Section A is a diagram representing 40 divisional drawers in alphabetic file, numbered 1 through 40. Below in Section B is a list of 30 names to be filed, numbered 1 through 30, with a drawer number opposite each name, representing the drawer in which it is assumed a file clerk has filed the name.

Determine which are filed CORRECTLY and which are filed INCORRECTLY based on standard rules for indexing and filing. If the name is filed CORRECTLY, print in the space at the right the letter C. If the name is filed INCORRECTLY, print in the space at the right the letter I.

SECTION A

1 Aa-Al	6 Bs-Bz	11 Ea-Er	16 Gp-Gz	21 Kp-Kz	26 Mo-Mz	31 Qa-Qz	36 Ta-Ti
2 Am-Au	7 Ca-Ch	12 Es-Ez	17 Ha-Hz	22 La-Le	27 Na-Nz	32 Ra-Rz	37 Tj-Tz
3 Av-Az	8 Ci-Co	13 Fa-Fr	18 Ia-Iz	23 Lf-Lz	28 Oa-Oz	33 Sa-Si	38 U-V
4 Ba-Bi	9 Cp-Cz	14 Fa-Fz	19 Ja-Jz	24 Ma-Mi	29 Pa-Pr	34 Sj-St	39 Wa-Wz
5 Bj-Br	10 Da-Dz	15 Ga-Go	20 Ka-Ko	25 Mj-Mo	30 Ps-Pz	35 Su-Sz	40 X-Y-Z

SECTION B

	Name or Title	Drawer No.	
1.	William O'Dea	28	1._____
2.	J. Arthur Crawford	8	2._____
3.	DuPont Chemical Co.	10	3._____
4.	Arnold Bros. Mfg. Co.	2	4._____
5.	Dr. Charles Ellis	10	5._____
6.	Gray and Doyle Adv. Agency	16	6._____
7.	Tom's Smoke Shop	37	7._____
8.	Wm. E. Jarrett Motor Corp.	39	8._____
9.	Penn-York Air Service	29	9._____
10.	Corinne La Fleur	13	10._____
11.	Cartright, Incorporated	7	11._____

2 (#9)

12.	7th Ave. Market	24	12._____
13.	Ft. Schuyler Apts.	13	13._____
14.	Madame Louise	23	14._____
15.	Commerce Dept., U.S. Govt.	38	15._____
16.	Norman Bulwer-Lytton	6	16._____
17.	Hilton Memorial Library	17	17._____
18.	The Linen Chest Gift Shop	36	18._____
19.	Ready Mix Supply Co.	32	19._____
20.	City Service Taxi	8	20._____
21.	A.R.C. Transportation Co.	37	21._____
22.	New Jersey Insurance Co.	19	22._____
23.	Capt. Larry Keith	20	23._____
24.	Girl Scouts Council	15	24._____
25.	University of Michigan	24	25._____
26.	Sister Ursula	38	26._____
27.	Am. Legion Post #9	22	27._____
28.	Board of Hudson River Reg. Dist.	17	28._____
29.	Mid West Bus Lines	39	29._____
30.	South West Tours, Inc.	34	30._____

KEY (CORRECT ANSWERS)

1.	C	11.	C	21.	I
2.	I	12.	I	22.	I
3.	C	13.	C	23.	C
4.	C	14.	I	24.	C
5.	I	15.	C	25.	I
6.	C	16.	C	26.	I
7.	C	17.	C	27.	I
8.	I	18.	I	28.	C
9.	C	19.	C	29.	I
10.	I	20.	C	30.	C

TEST 10

DIRECTIONS: Each question or incomplete statement is followed by several suggested answers or completions. Select the one that BEST answers the question or completes the statement. *PRINT THE LETTER OF THE CORRECT ANSWER IN THE SPACE AT THE RIGHT.*

1. Of the following statements about the numeric system of filing, the one which is CORRECT is that it
   A. is the least accurate of all methods of filing
   B. eliminates the need for cross-referencing
   C. allows for very limited expansion
   D. requires a separate index

   1.____

2. When more than one name or subject is involved in a piece of correspondence to be filed, the office assistant should GENERALLY
   A. prepare a cross-reference sheet
   B. establish a geographical filing system
   C. prepare out-guides
   D. establish a separate index card for noting such correspondence

   2.____

3. A tickler file is MOST generally used for
   A. identification of material contained in a numeric file
   B. maintenance of a current listing of telephone numbers
   C. follow-up of matters requiring future attention
   D. control of records borrowed or otherwise removed from the file

   3.____

4. In filing, the name Ms. "Ann Catalana-Moss" should GENERALLY be indexed as
   A. Moss, Catalana, Ann (Ms.)   B. Catalana-Moss, Ann (Ms.)
   C. Ann Catalana-Moss (Ms.)   D. Moss-Catalana, Ann (Ms.)

   4.____

5. An office assistant has a set of four cards, each of which contains one of the following names.
   In alphabetic filing, the FIRST of the cards to be filed is
   A. (Ms.) Alma John
   B. Mrs. John (Patricia) Edwards
   C. John-Edward School Supplies, Inc.
   D. John H. Edwards

   5.____

6. Generally, of the following, the name to be filed FIRST in an alphabetical filing system is
   A. Diane Maestro   B. Diana McElroy
   C. James Mackell   D. James McKell

   6.____

7. According to generally recognized rules of filing in an alphabetic filing system, the one of the following names which normally should be filed LAST is
   A. Department of Education, New York State
   B. F. B. I.
   C. Police Department of New York City
   D. P.S. 81 of New York City

7.____

KEY (CORRECT ANSWERS)

1. D
2. A
3. C
4. B
5. D
6. C
7. B

NAME AND NUMBER CHECKING
EXAMINATION SECTION
TEST 1

DIRECTIONS: This test is designed to measure your speed/and accuracy. You are urged to work both quickly and accurately and to do correctly as many lists as you can in the time allowed. The test consists of lists or pairs of names and numbers. Count the number of IDENTICAL pairs in each list. Then, select the correct number, 1, 2, 3, 4, 5, and indicate your choice in the space at the right. Two sample questions are presented for your guidance, together with the correct solutions.

SAMPLE LIST A
Adelphi College – Adelphia College
Braxton Corp – Braxeton Corp.
Wassaic State School – Wassaic State School
Central Islip State Hospital – Central Isllip State Hospital
Greenwich House – Greenwich House

NOTE: There are only two correct pairs—Wassaic State School and Greenwich House. Therefore, the CORRECT answer is 2.

SAMPLE LIST B
78453694 – 78453684
784530 – 784530
533 – 534
67845 – 67845
2368745 – 2368755

NOTE: There are only two correct pairs—784530 and 67845. Therefore, the CORRECT answer is 2.

LIST 1   1.____
    Diagnostic Clinic   – Diagnostic Clinic
    Yorkville Health   – Yorkville Health
    Meinhard Clinic   – Meinhart Clinic
    Corlears Clinic   – Carlears Clinic
    Tremont Diagnostic   – Tremont Diagnostic

LIST 2   2.____
    73526   – 73526
    7283627198   – 7283627198
    627   – 637
    728352617283   – 7283526178282
    6281   – 6281

LIST 3
- Jefferson Clinic — Jeffersen Clinic
- Mott Haven Center — Mott Havan Center
- Bronx Hospital — Bronx Hospital
- Montefiore Hospital — Montifeore Hospital
- Beth Isreal Hospital — Beth Israel Hospital

3.____

LIST 4
- 936271826 — 936371826
- 5271 — 5291
- 82637192037 — 82637192037
- 527182 — 5271882
- 726354256 - 72635456

4.____

LIST 5
- Trinity Hospital — Trinity Hospital
- Central Harlem — Centrel Harlem
- St. Luke's Hospital — St. Lukes' Hospital
- Mt. Sinai Hospital — Mt. Sinia Hospital
- N.Y. Dispensery — N.Y. Dispensary

5.____

LIST 6
- 725361552637 — 725361555637
- 7526378 — 7526377
- 6975 — 6975
- 82637481028 — 82637481028
- 3427 — 3429

6.____

LIST 7
- Misericordia Hospital — Miseracordia Hospital
- Lebonan Hospital — Lebanon Hospital
- Gouverneur Hospital — Gouverner Hospital
- German Polyclinic — German Policlinic
- French Hospital — French Hospital

7.____

LIST 8
- 8277364933251 — 827364933351
- 63728 — 63728
- 367281 — 367281
- 62733846273 — 6273846293
- 62836 - 6283

8.____

LIST 9
- King's County Hospital — Kings County Hospital
- St. Johns Long Island — St. John's Long Island
- Bellevue Hospital — Bellvue Hospital
- Beth David Hospital — Beth David Hospital
- Samaritan Hospital — Samariton Hospital

9.____

LIST 10   10.____
    62836454   – 62836455
    42738267   – 42738369
    573829   – 573829
    738291627874   – 738291627874
    725   - 735

LIST 11   11.____
    Bloomingdal Clinic   – Bloomingdale Clinic
    Communitty Hospital – Community Hospital
    Metroplitan Hospital – Metropoliton Hospital
    Lenox Hill Hospital   – Lonex Hill Hospital
    Lincoln Hospital   – Lincoln Hospital

LIST 12   12.____
    6283364728   – 6283648
    627385   – 627383
    54283902   – 54283602
    63354   – 63354
    7283562781   - 7283562781

LIST 13   13.____
    Sydenham Hospital   – Sydanham Hospital
    Roosevalt Hospital   – Roosevelt Hospital
    Vanderbilt Clinic   – Vanderbild Clinic
    Women's Hospital   – Woman's Hospital
    Flushing Hospital   – Flushing Hospital

LIST 14   14.____
    62738   – 62738
    727355542321   – 72735542321
    263849332   – 263849332
    262837   – 263837
    47382912   - 47382922

LIST 15   15.____
    Episcopal Hospital   – Episcapal Hospital
    Flower Hospital   – Flouer Hospital
    Stuyvesent Clinic   – Stuyvesant Clinic
    Jamaica Clinic   – Jamaica Clinic
    Ridgwood Clinic   – Ridgewood Clinic

LIST 16   16.____
    628367299   – 628367399
    111   – 111
    118293304829   – 1182839489
    4448   – 4448
    333693678   - 333693678

4 (#1)

LIST 17　　　　　　　　　　　　　　　　　　　　　　　　　　　　　　　　　17.____
    Arietta Crane Farm — Areitta Crane Farm
    Bikur Chilim Home — Bikur Chilom Home
    Burke Foundation — Burke Foundation
    Blythedale Home — Blythdale Home
    Campbell Cottages — Cambell Cottages

LIST 18　　　　　　　　　　　　　　　　　　　　　　　　　　　　　　　　　18.____
    32123 — 32132
    273893326783 — 27389326783
    473829 — 473829
    7382937 — 7383937
    3628890122332 — 36289012332

LIST 19　　　　　　　　　　　　　　　　　　　　　　　　　　　　　　　　　19.____
    Caraline Rest — Caroline Rest
    Loreto Rest — Loretto Rest
    Edgewater Creche — Edgwater Creche
    Holiday Farm — Holiday Farm
    House of St. Giles — House of st. Giles

LIST 20　　　　　　　　　　　　　　　　　　　　　　　　　　　　　　　　　20.____
    557286777 — 55728677
    3678902 — 3678892
    1567839 — 1567839
    7865434712 — 7865344712
    9927382 — 9927382

LIST 21　　　　　　　　　　　　　　　　　　　　　　　　　　　　　　　　　21.____
    Isabella Home — Isabela Home
    James A. Moore Home — James A. More Home
    The Robin's Nest — The Roben's Nest
    Pelham Home — Pelam Home
    St. Eleanora's Home — St. Eleanora's Home

LIST 22　　　　　　　　　　　　　　　　　　　　　　　　　　　　　　　　　22.____
    273648293048 — 273648293048
    334 — 334
    7362536478 — 7362536478
    7362819273 — 7362819273
    7362 — 7363

LIST 23　　　　　　　　　　　　　　　　　　　　　　　　　　　　　　　　　23.____
    St. Pheobe's Mission — St. Phebe's Mission
    Seaside Home — Seaside Home
    Speedwell Society — Speedwell Society
    Valeria Home — Valera Home
    Wiltwyck — Wildwyck

5 (#1)

LIST 24
    63728   – 63738
    63728192736   – 63728192738
    428   – 458
    62738291527   – 62738291529
    63728192   - 63728192

24.____

LIST 25
    McGaffin   – McGafin
    David Ardslee   – David Ardslee
    Axton Supply   – Axeton Supply Co
    Alice Russell   – Alice Russell
    Dobson Mfg. Co.   – Dobsen Mfg. Co.

25.____

KEY (CORRECT ANSWERS)

1.	3	11.	1
2.	3	12.	2
3.	1	13.	1
4.	1	14.	2
5.	1	15.	1
6.	2	16.	3
7.	1	17.	1
8.	2	18.	1
9.	1	19.	1
10.	2	20.	2

21.	1
22.	4
23.	2
24.	1
25.	2

TEST 2

DIRECTIONS: This test is designed to measure your speed/and accuracy. You are urged to work both quickly and accurately and to do correctly as many lists as you can in the time allowed. The test consists of lists or pairs of names and numbers. Count the number of IDENTICAL pairs in each list. Then, select the correct number, 1, 2, 3, 4, 5, and indicate your choice in the space at the right.

LIST 1   1.____
    82637381028   – 82637281028
    928   – 928
    72937281028   – 72937281028
    7362   – 7362
    927382615   – 927382615

LIST 2   2.____
    Albee Theatre   – Albee Theatre
    Lapland Lumber Co.   – Laplund Lumber Co.
    Adelphi College   – Adelphi College
    Jones & Son Inc.   – Jones & Sons Inc.
    S.W. Ponds Co.   – S.W. Ponds Co.

LIST 3   3.____
    85345   – 85345
    895643278   – 895643277
    726352   – 726353
    632685   – 632685
    7263524   – 7236524

LIST 4   4.____
    Eagle Library   – Eagle Library
    Dodge Ltd.   – Dodge Co.
    Stromberg Carlson   – Stromberg Carlsen
    Clairice Ling   – Clairice Linng
    Mason Book Co.   – Matson Book Co.

LIST 5   5.____
    66273   – 66273
    629   – 629
    7382517283   – 7382517283
    637281   – 639281
    2738261   – 2788261

LIST 6   6.____
    Robert MacColl   – Robert McColl
    Buick Motor   – Buck Motors
    Murray Bay & Co. Ltd.   – Murray Bay Co. Ltd.
    L.T. Ltyle   – L.T. Lyttle
    A.S. Landas   – A.S. Landas

LIST 7
    6271526374890   – 627152637490
    73526189   – 73526189
    5372   – 5392
    637281142   – 63728124
    4783946   – 4783046

7.____

LIST 8
    Tyndall Burke   – Tyndell Burke
    W. Briehl   – W. Briehl
    Burritt Publishing Co.   – Buritt Publishing Co.
    Frederick Breyer & Co.   – Frederick Breyer Co.
    Bailey Buulard   – Bailey Bullard

8.____

LIST 9
    634   – 634
    16837   – 163837
    273892223678   – 27389223678
    527182   – 527782
    3628901223   – 3629002223

9.____

LIST 10
    Ernest Boas   – Ernest Boas
    Rankin Barne   – Rankin Barnes
    Edward Appley   – Edward Appely
    Camel   – Camel
    Caiger Food Co.   – Caiger Food Co.

10.____

LIST 11
    6273   – 6273
    322   – 332
    15672839   – 15672839
    63728192637   – 63728192639
    738   – 738

11.____

LIST 12
    Wells Fargo Co.   – Wells Fargo Co.
    W.D. Brett   – W.D. Britt
    Tassco Co.   – Tassko Co.
    Republic Mills   – Republic Mill
    R.W. Burnham   – R.W. Burhnam

12.____

LIST 13
    7253529152   – 7283529152
    6283   – 6383
    52839102738   – 5283910238
    308   – 398
    82637201927   – 8263720127

13.____

LIST 14
    Schumacker Co.   – Shumacker Co.
    C.H. Caiger   – C.H. Caiger
    Abraham Strauss   – Abram Straus
    B.F. Boettjer   – B.F. Boettijer
    Cut-Rate Store   – Cut-Rate Stores

14.____

LIST 15
    15273826   – 15273826
    72537   – 73537
    726391027384   – 62639107384
    637389   – 627399
    725382910   – 725382910

15.____

LIST 16
    Hixby Ltd.   – Hixby Lt'd.
    S. Reiner   – S. Riener
    Reynard Co.   – Reynord Co.
    Esso Gassoline Co. – Esso Gasolene Co.
    Belle Brock   – Belle Brock

16.____

LIST 17
    7245   – 7245
    819263728192   – 819263728172
    682537289   – 682537298
    789   – 789
    82936542891   – 82936542891

17.____

LIST 18
    Joseph Cartwright   – Joseph Cartwrite
    Foote Food Co.   – Foot Food Co.
    Weiman & Held   – Weiman & Held
    Sanderson Shoe Co. – Sandersen Shoe Co.
    A.M. Byrne   – A.N. Byrne

18.____

LIST 19
    4738267   – 4738277
    63728   – 63729
    6283628901   – 6283628991
    918264   – 918264
    263728192037   – 2637728192073

19.____

LIST 20
    Exray Laboratories – Exray Labratories
    Curley Toy Co.   – Curly Toy Co.
    J. Lauer & Cross   – J. Laeur & Cross
    Mireco Brands   – Mireco Brands
    Sandor Lorand   – Sandor Larand

20.____

4 (#2)

LIST 21   21.____
   607   – 609
   6405   – 6403
   976   – 996
   101267   – 101267
   2065432   – 20965432

LIST 22   22.____
   John Macy & Sons   – John Macy & Son
   Venus Pencil Co.   – Venus Pencil Co.
   Nell McGinnis   – Nell McGinnis
   McCutcheon & Co.   – McCutcheon & Co.
   Sun-Tan Oil   – Sun-Tan Oil

LIST 23   23.____
   703345700   – 703345700
   46754   – 466754
   3367490   – 3367490
   3379   – 3778
   47384   – 47394

LIST 24   24.____
   arthritis   – arthritis
   asthma   – asthma
   endocrine   – endocrene
   gastro-enterological – gastrol-enteralogical
   orthopedic   – orthopedic

LIST 25   25.____
   743829432   – 743828432
   998   – 998
   732816253902 – 732816252902
   46829   – 46830
   7439120249   – 7439210249

KEY (CORRECT ANSWERS)

1.	4		11.	3
2.	3		12.	1
3.	2		13.	1
4.	1		14.	1
5.	2		15.	2
6.	1		16.	1
7.	2		17.	3
8.	1		18.	1
9.	1		19.	1
10.	3		20.	1

21. 1
22. 4
23. 2
24. 3
25. 1

EXAMINATION SECTION

TEST 1

DIRECTIONS: Each question or incomplete statement is followed by several suggested answers or completions. Select the one that BEST answers the question or completes the statement. *PRINT THE LETTER OF THE CORRECT ANSWER IN THE SPACE AT THE RIGHT.*

Questions 1-22.

DIRECTIONS: Read through each group of words. Indicate in the space at the right the letter of the misspelled word.

1. A. miniature B. recession 1.____
   C. accommodate D. supress

2. A. mortgage B. illogical 2.____
   C. fasinate D. pronounce

3. A. calendar B. heros 3.____
   C. ecstasy D. librarian

4. A. initiative B. extraordinary 4.____
   C. villian D. exaggerate

5. A. absence B. sense 5.____
   C. dosn't D. height

6. A. curiosity B. ninety 6.____
   C. truely D. grammar

7. A. amateur B. definate 7.____
   C. meant D. changeable

8. A. excellent B. studioes 8.____
   C. achievement D. weird

9. A. goverment B. description 9.____
   C. sergeant D. desirable

10. A. proceed B. anxious 10.____
    C. neice D. precede

11. A. environment B. omitted 11.____
    C. apparant D. misconstrue

12. A. comparative B. hindrance 12.____
    C. benefited D. unamimous

13. A. embarrass B. recommend 13.____
    C. desciple D. argument

14. A. sophomore B. suprintendent 14.____
    C. concievable D. disastrous

15. A. agressive B. questionnaire 15.____
    C. occurred D. rhythm

16. A. peaceable B. conscientious 16.____
    C. redicule D. deterrent

17. A. mischievious B. writing 17.____
    C. competition D. athletics

18. A. auxiliary B. synonymous 18.____
    C. maneuver D. repitition

19. A. existence B. optimistic 19.____
    C. acquitted D. tragedy

20. A. hypocrisy B. parrallel 20.____
    C. exhilaration D. prevalent

21. A. convalesence B. infallible 21.____
    C. destitute D. grotesque

22. A. magnanimity B. asassination 22.____
    C. incorrigible D. pestilence

Questions 23-40.

DIRECTIONS: In Questions 23 through 40, one sentence fragment contains an error in punctuation or capitalization. Indicate the letter of the INCORRECT sentence fragment and place it in the space at the right.

23. A. Despite a year's work 23.____
    B. in a well-equipped laboratory
    C. my Uncle failed to complete his research
    D. now he will never graduate.

24. A. Gene, if you are going to sleep 24.____
    B. all afternoon I will enter
    C. that ladies' golf tournament
    D. sponsored by the Chamber of Commerce.

3 (#1)

25. A. Seeing the cat slink toward the barn,
    B. the farmer's wife jumped off the
    C. ladder picked up a broom, and began
    D. shouting at the top of her voice.

    25._____

26. A. Extending over southeast Idaho and
    B. northwest Wyoming, the Tetons
    C. are noted for their height; however the
    D. highest peak is actually under 14,000 feet.

    26._____

27. A. "Sarah, can you recall the name
    B. of the English queen
    C. who supposedly said, 'We are not
    D. amused?"

    27._____

28. A. My aunt's graduation present to me
    B. cost, I imagine more than she could
    C. actually afford. It's a
    D. Swiss watch with numerous features.

    28._____

29. A. On the left are examples of buildings
    B. from the Classical Period; two temples
    C. one of which was dedicated to Zeus; the
    D. Agora, a marketplace; and a large arch.

    29._____

30. A. Tired of sonic booms, the people who
    B. live near Springfield's Municipal Airport
    C. formed an anti noise organization
    D. with the amusing name of Sound Off.

    30._____

31. A. "Joe, Mrs. Sweeney said, "your family
    B. arrives Sunday. Since you'll be in
    C. the Labor Day parade, we could ask Mr.
    D. Krohn, who has a big car, to meet them."

    31._____

32. A. The plumber emerged from the basement and
    B. said, "Mr. Cohen I found the trouble in
    C. your water heater. Could you move those
    D. Schwinn bikes out of my way?"

    32._____

33. A. The President walked slowly to the
    B. podium, bowed to Edward Everett Hale
    C. the other speaker, and began his formal address:
    D. "Fourscore and seven years ago...."

    33._____

34. A. Mr. Fontana, I hope, will arrive before
    B. the beginning of the ceremonies; however,
    C. if his plane is delayed, I have a substitute
    D. speaker who can be here at a moments' notice.

    34._____

35. A. Gladys wedding dress, a satin creation,
    B. lay crumpled on the floor; her veil,
    C. torn and streaked, lay nearby. "Jilted!"
    D. shrieked Gladys. She was clearly annoyed.

35.____

36. A. Although it is poor grammar, the word
    B. hopefully has become television's newest
    C. pet expression; I hope (to use the correct
    D. form) that it will soon pass from favor.

36.____

37. A.   Plaza Apartment Hotel
    B.   103 Tower road
    C.   Hampstead, Iowa 52025
    D.   March 13, 2021

37.____

38. A. Circulation Department
    B. British History Illustrated
    C. 3000 Walnut Street
    D. Boulder Colorado 80302

38.____

39. A. Dear Sirs:
    B. Last spring I ordered a subscription to your
    C. magazine. I had read and enjoyed the May
    D. issue containing the article titled "kings."

39.____

40. A. I have not however, received a
    B. single issue. Will you check this?
    C. Sincerely,
    D. Maria Herrera

40.____

Questions 41-70.

DIRECTIONS: Questions 41 through 70 represent common grammatical concerns: subject-verb agreement, appropriate use of pronouns, and appropriate use of verbs. Read each sentence and indicate the letter of the grammatically CORRECT answer in the space at the right.

41. THE REIVERS, one of William Faulkner's last works, _____ made into a movie starring Steve McQueen.
    A. has been   B. have been   C. are being   D. were

41.____

42. He _____ on the ground, his eyes fastened on an ant slowly pushing a morsel of food toward the ant hill.
    A. layed   B. laid   C. had laid   D. lay

42.____

43. Nobody in the tri-cities _____ to admit that a flood could be disastrous.
    A. are willing   B. have been willing
    C. is willing   D. were willing

43.____

44. "_____," the senator asked, "have you convinced to run against the incumbent?"
    A. Who   B. Whom   C. Whomever   D. Womsoever

45. Of all the psychology courses that I took, Statistics 101 _____ the most demanding.
    A. was   B. are   C. is   D. were

46. Neither the conductor nor the orchestra members _____ the music to be applauded so enthusiastically.
    A. were expecting
    B. was expecting
    C. is expected
    D. has been expecting

47. The requirements for admission to the Lettermen's Club _____ posted outside the athletic director's office for months.
    A. was   B. was being   C. has been   D. have been

48. Please give me a list of the people _____ to compete in the kayak race.
    A. whom you think have planned
    B. who you think has planned
    C. who you think is planning
    D. who you think are planning

49. I saw Eloise and Abelard earlier today; _____ were riding around in a fancy 1956 MG.
    A. she and him   B. her and him   C. she and he   D. her and he

50. If you _____ the trunk in the attic, I'll unpack it later today.
    A. can sit
    B. are able to sit
    C. can set
    D. have sat

51. _____ all of the flour been used, or may I borrow three cups?
    A. Have   B. Has   C. Is   D. Could

52. In exasperation, the cycle shop's owner suggested that _____ there too long.
    A. us boys were
    B. we boys were
    C. us boys had been
    D. we boys had been

53. Idleness as well as money _____ the root of all evil.
    A. have been
    B. were to have been
    C. is
    D. are

54. Only the string players from the quartet—Gregory, Isaac, _____—remained after the concert to answer questions.
    A. him, and I
    B. he, and I
    C. him, and me
    D. he, and me

55. Of all the antiques that _____ for sale, Gertrude chose to buy a stupid glass thimble.
    A. was
    B. is
    C. would have
    D. were

56. The detective snapped, "Don't confuse me with theories about _____ you believe committed the crime!"
    A. who   B. whom   C. whomever   D. which

57. _____ when we first called, we might have avoided our present predicament.
    A. The plumber's coming
    B. If the plumber would have come
    C. If the plumber had come
    D. If the plumber was to have come

58. We thought the sun _____ in the north until we discovered that our compass was defective.
    A. had rose
    B. had risen
    C. had rised
    D. had raised

59. Each play of Shakespeare's _____ more than _____ share of memorable characters.
    A. contain its
    B. contains; its
    C. contains; it's
    D. contain; their

60. Our English teacher suggested to _____ seniors that either Tolstoy or Dickens _____ the outstanding novelist of the nineteenth century.
    A. we; was considered
    B. we; were considered
    C. us; was considered
    D. us; were considered

61. Sherlock Holmes, together with his great friend and companion Dr. Watson, _____ to aid the woman _____ had stumbled into the room.
    A. has agreed; who
    B. have agreed; whom
    C. has agreed; whom
    D. have agreed; who

62. Several of the deer _____ when they spotted my backpack _____ open in the meadow.
    A. was frightened; laying
    B. were frightened; lying
    C. were frightened; laying
    D. was frightened; lying

63. After the Scholarship Committee announces _____ selection, hysterics often _____.
    A. it's; occur
    B. its; occur
    C. their; occur
    D. their; occurs

64. I _____ the key on the table last night so you and _____ could find it.
    A. layed; her
    B. lay; she
    C. laid; she
    D. laid; her

65. Some of the antelope _____ wandered away from the meadow where the rancher _____ the block of salt.
    A. has; sat
    B. has; set
    C. have; had set
    D. has; sets

66. Macaroni and cheese _____ best to us (that is, to Andy and _____) when Mother adds extra cheddar cheese.
    A. tastes; I
    B. tastes; me
    C. taste; me
    D. taste; I

66.____

67. Frank said, "It must have been _____ called the phone company."
    A. she who
    B. she whom
    C. her who
    D. her whom

67.____

68. The herd _____ moving restlessly at every bolt of lightning; it was either Ted or _____ who saw the beginning of the stampede.
    A. was; me
    B. were; I
    C. was; I
    D. have been; me

68.____

69. The foreman _____ his lateness by saying that his alarm clock _____ until six minutes before eight.
    A. explains; had not rang
    B. explained; has not rung
    C. has explained; rung
    D. explained; hadn't rung

69.____

70. Of all the coaches, Ms. Cox is the only one who _____ that Sherry dives more gracefully than _____.
    A. is always saying; I
    B. is always saying; me
    C. are always saying; I
    D. were always saying; me

70.____

Questions 71-90.

DIRECTIONS: Choose the word in Questions 71 through 90 that is MOST opposite in meaning to the italicized word.

71. *fact*
    A. statistic
    B. statement
    C. incredible
    D. conjecture

71.____

72. *stiff*
    A. fastidious
    B. babble
    C. supple
    D. apprehensive

72.____

73. *blunt*
    A. concise
    B. tactful
    C. artistic
    D. humble

73.____

74. *foreign*
    A. pertinent
    B. comely
    C. strange
    D. scrupulous

74.____

75. *anger*
    A. infer
    B. pacify
    C. taint
    D. revile

75.____

76. *frank*
    A. earnest
    B. reticent
    C. post
    D. expensive

76.____

77. *secure*
    A. precarious   B. acquire   C. moderate   D. frenzied

78. *petty*
    A. harmonious   B. careful
    C. forthright   D. momentous

79. *concede*
    A. dispute   B. reciprocate
    C. subvert   D. propagate

80. *benefit*
    A. liquidation   B. bazaar
    C. detriment   D. profit

81. *capricious*
    A. preposterous   B. constant
    C. diabolical   D. careless

82. *boisterous*
    A. devious   B. valiant   C. girlish   D. taciturn

83. *harmony*
    A. congruence   B. discord   C. chagrin   D. melody

84. *laudable*
    A. auspicious   B. despicable
    C. acclaimed   D. doubtful

85. *adherent*
    A. partisan   B. stoic   C. renegade   D. recluse

86. *exuberant*
    A. frail   B. corpulent   C. austere   D. bigot

87. *spurn*
    A. accede   B. flail   C. efface   D. annihilate

88. *spontaneous*
    A. hapless   B. corrosive
    C. intentional   D. willful

89. *disparage*
    A. abolish   B. exude   C. incriminate   D. extol

90. *timorous*
    A. succinct   B. chaste   C. audacious   D. insouciant

KEY (CORRECT ANSWERS)

1. D	21. A	41. A	61. A	81. B
2. C	22. B	42. D	62.	82. D
3. B	23. C	43. C	63. B	83. B
4. C	24. B	44. B	64. C	84. B
5. C	25. C	45. A	65. C	85. C
6. C	26. C	46. A	66. B	86. C
7. B	27. D	47. D	67. A	87. A
8. B	28. B	48. A	68. C	88. C
9. A	29. B	49. C	69. D	89. D
10. C	30. C	50. C	70. A	90. C
11. C	31. A	51. B	71. D	
12. D	32. B	52. D	72. C	
13. C	33. B	53. C	73. B	
14. C	34. D	54. B	74. A	
15. A	35. A	55. D	75. B	
16. C	36. B	56. B	76. B	
17. A	37. B	57. C	77. A	
18. D	38. D	58. B	78. D	
19. B	39. D	59. B	79. A	
20. B	40. A	60. C	80. C	

PHILOSOPHY, PRINCIPLES, PRACTICES, AND TECHNICS
OF
SUPERVISION, ADMINISTRATION, MANAGEMENT, AND ORGANIZATION

TABLE OF CONTENTS

	Page
MEANING OF SUPERVISION	1
THE OLD AND THE NEW SUPERVISION	1
THE EIGHT (8) BASIC PRINCIPLES OF THE NEW SUPERVISION	1
I. Principle of Responsibility	1
II. Principle of Authority	2
III. Principle of Self-Growth	2
IV. Principle of Individual Worth	2
V. Principle of Creative Leadership	2
VI. Principle of Success and Failure	2
VII. Principle of Science	3
VIII. Principle of Cooperation	3
WHAT IS ADMINISTRATION?	3
I. Practices Commonly Classed as "Supervisory"	3
II. Practices Commonly Classed as "Administrative"	3
III. Practices Commonly Classed as Both "Supervisory" and "Administrative"	4
RESPONSIBILITIES OF THE SUPERVISOR	4
COMPETENCIES OF THE SUPERVISOR	4
THE PROFESSIONAL SUPERVISOR-EMPLOYEE RELATIONSHIP	4
MINI-TEXT IN SUPERVISION, ADMINISTRATION, MANAGEMENT, AND ORGANIZATION	5
I. Brief Highlights	5
A. Levels of Management	6
B. What the Supervisor Must Learn	6
C. A Definition of Supervision	6
D. Elements of the Team Concept	6
E. Principles of Organization	6
F. The Four Important Parts of Every Job	7
G. Principles of Delegation	7
H. Principles of Effective Communications	7
I. Principles of Work Improvement	7
J. Areas of Job Improvement	7
K. Seven Key Points in Making Improvements	8

L.	Corrective Techniques for Job Improvement	8
M.	A Planning Checklist	8
N.	Five Characteristics of Good Directions	9
O.	Types of Directions	9
P.	Controls	9
Q.	Orienting the New Employee	9
R.	Checklist for Orienting New Employees	9
S.	Principles of Learning	10
T.	Causes of Poor Performance	10
U.	Four Major Steps in On-the-Job Instructions	10
V.	Employees Want Five Things	10
W.	Some Don'ts in Regard to Praise	11
X.	How to Gain Your Workers' Confidence	11
Y.	Sources of Employee Problems	11
Z.	The Supervisor's Key to Discipline	11
AA.	Five Important Processes of Management	12
BB.	When the Supervisor Fails to Plan	12
CC.	Fourteen General Principles of Management	12
DD.	Change	12

II. Brief Topical Summaries — 13
   A. Who/What is the Supervisor? — 13
   B. The Sociology of Work — 13
   C. Principles and Practices of Supervision — 14
   D. Dynamic Leadership — 14
   E. Processes for Solving Problems — 15
   F. Training for Results — 15
   G. Health, Safety, and Accident Prevention — 16
   H. Equal Employment Opportunity — 16
   I. Improving Communications — 16
   J. Self-Development — 17
   K. Teaching and Training — 17
      1. The Teaching Process — 17
          a. Preparation — 17
          b. Presentation — 18
          c. Summary — 18
          d. Application — 18
          e. Evaluation — 18
      2. Teaching Methods — 18
          a. Lecture — 18
          b. Discussion — 18
          c. Demonstration — 19
          d. Performance — 19
          e. Which Method to Use — 19

PHILOSOPHY, PRINCIPLES, PRACTICES, AND TECHNICS OF SUPERVISION, ADMINISTRATION, MANAGEMENT, AND ORGANIZATION

MEANING OF SUPERVISION

The extension of the democratic philosophy has been accompanied by an extension in the scope of supervision. Modern leaders and supervisors no longer think of supervision in the narrow sense of being confined chiefly to visiting employees, supplying materials, or rating the staff. They regard supervision as being intimately related to all the concerned agencies of society, they speak of the supervisor's function in terms of "growth," rather than the "improvement" of employees.

This modern concept of supervision may be defined as follows: Supervision is leadership and the development of leadership within groups which are cooperatively engaged in inspection, research, training, guidance, and evaluation.

THE OLD AND THE NEW SUPERVISION

TRADITIONAL
1. Inspection
2. Focused on the employee
3. Visitation
4. Random and haphazard
5. Imposed and authoritarian
6. One person usually

MODERN
1. Study and analysis
2. Focused on aims, materials, methods, supervisors, employees, environment
3. Demonstrations, intervisitation, workshops, directed reading, bulletins, etc.
4. Definitely organized and planned (scientific)
5. Cooperative and democratic
6. Many persons involved (creative)

THE EIGHT (8) BASIC PRINCIPLES OF THE NEW SUPERVISION

I. Principle of Responsibility
   Authority to act and responsibility for acting must be joined.
   A. If you give responsibility, give authority.
   B. Define employee duties clearly.
   C. Protect employees from criticism by others.
   D. Recognize the rights as well as obligations of employees.
   E. Achieve the aims of a democratic society insofar as it is possible within the area of your work.
   F. Establish a situation favorable to training and learning.
   G. Accept ultimate responsibility for everything done in your section, unit, office, division, department.
   H. Good administration and good supervision are inseparable.

II. Principle of Authority
The success of the supervisor is measured by the extent to which the power of authority is not used.
   A. Exercise simplicity and informality in supervision
   B. Use the simplest machinery of supervision
   C. If it is good for the organization as a whole, it is probably justified.
   D. Seldom be arbitrary or authoritative.
   E. Do not base your work on the power of position or of personality.
   F. Permit and encourage the free expression of opinions.

III. Principle of Self-Growth
The success of the supervisor is measured by the extent to which, and the speed with which, he is no longer needed.
   A. Base criticism on principles, not on specifics.
   B. Point out higher activities to employees.
   C. Train for self-thinking by employees to meet new situations.
   D. Stimulate initiative, self-reliance, and individual responsibility
   E. Concentrate on stimulating the growth of employees rather than on removing defects.

IV. Principle of Individual Worth
Respect for the individual is a paramount consideration in supervision.
   A. Be human and sympathetic in dealing with employees.
   B. Don't nag about things to be done.
   C. Recognize the individual differences among employees and seek opportunities to permit best expression of each personality.

V. Principle of Creative Leadership
The best supervision is that which is not apparent to the employee.
   A. Stimulate, don't drive employees to creative action.
   B. Emphasize doing good things.
   C. Encourage employees to do what they do best.
   D. Do not be too greatly concerned with details of subject or method.
   E. Do not be concerned exclusively with immediate problems and activities.
   F. Reveal higher activities and make them both desired and maximally possible.
   G. Determine procedures in the light of each situation but see that these are derived from a sound basic philosophy.
   H. Aid, inspire, and lead so as to liberate the creative spirit latent in all good employees.

VI. Principle of Success and Failure
There are no unsuccessful employees, only unsuccessful supervisors who have failed to give proper leadership.
   A. Adapt suggestions to the capacities, attitudes, and prejudices of employees.
   B. Be gradual, be progressive, be persistent.
   C. Help the employee find the general principle; have the employee apply his own problem to the general principle.
   D. Give adequate appreciation for good work and honest effort.
   E. Anticipate employee difficulties and help to prevent them.
   F. Encourage employees to do the desirable things they will do anyway.
   G. Judge your supervision by the results it secures.

VII. Principle of Science
Successful supervision is scientific, objective, and experimental. It is based on facts, not on prejudices.
   A.   Be cumulative in results.
   B.   Never divorce your suggestions from the goals of training.
   C.   Don't be impatient of results.
   D.   Keep all matters on a professional, not a personal, level.
   E.   Do not be concerned exclusively with immediate problems and activities.
   F.   Use objective means of determining achievement and rating where possible.

VIII. Principle of Cooperation
Supervision is a cooperative enterprise between supervisor and employee.
   A.   Begin with conditions as they are.
   B.   Ask opinions of all involved when formulating policies.
   C.   Organization is as good as its weakest link.
   D.   Let employees help to determine policies and department programs.
   E.   Be approachable and accessible—physically and mentally.
   F.   Develop pleasant social relationships.

WHAT IS ADMINISTRATION

Administration is concerned with providing the environment, the material facilities, and the operational procedures that will promote the maximum growth and development of supervisors and employees. (Organization is an aspect and a concomitant of administration.)

There is no sharp line of demarcation between supervision and administration; these functions are intimately interrelated and, often, overlapping. They are complementary activities.

I.   Practices Commonly Classed as "Supervisory"
   A.   Conducting employees' conferences
   B.   Visiting sections, units, offices, divisions, departments
   C.   Arranging for demonstrations
   D.   Examining plans
   E.   Suggesting professional reading
   F.   Interpreting bulletins
   G.   Recommending in-service training courses
   H.   Encouraging experimentation
   I.   Appraising employee morale
   J.   Providing for intervisitation

II. Practices Commonly Classified as "Administrative"
   A.   Management of the office
   B.   Arrangement of schedules for extra duties
   C.   Assignment of rooms or areas
   D.   Distribution of supplies
   E.   Keeping records and reports
   F.   Care of audio-visual materials
   G.   Keeping inventory records
   H.   Checking record cards and books

      I. Programming special activities
      J. Checking on the attendance and punctuality of employees

III. Practices Commonly Classified as Both "Supervisory" and "Administrative"
    A. Program construction
    B. Testing or evaluating outcomes
    C. Personnel accounting
    D. Ordering instructional materials

RESPONSIBILITIES OF THE SUPERVISOR

A person employed in a supervisory capacity must constantly be able to improve his own efficiency and ability. He represent the employer to the employees and only continuous self-examination can make him a capable supervisor.

Leadership and training are the supervisor's responsibility. An efficient working unit is one in which the employees work with the supervisor. It is his job to bring out the best in his employees. He must always be relaxed, courteous, and calm in his association with his employees. Their feelings are important, and a harsh attitude does not develop the most efficient employees.

COMPETENCES OF THE SUPERVISOR

    I. Complete knowledge of the duties and responsibilities of his position.
    II. To be able to organize a job, plan ahead, and carry through.
    III. To have self-confidence and initiative.
    IV. To be able to handle the unexpected situation and make quick decisions.
    V. To be able to properly train subordinates in the positions they are best suited for.
    VI. To be able to keep good human relations among his subordinates.
    VII. To be able to keep good human relations between his subordinates and himself and to earn their respect and trust.

THE PROFESSIONAL SUPERVISOR-EMPLOYEE RELATIONSHIP

There are two kinds of efficiency: one kind is only apparent and is produced in organizations through the exercise of mere discipline; this is but a simulation of the second, or true, efficiency which springs from spontaneous cooperation. If you are a manager, no matter how great or small your responsibility, it is your job, in the final analysis, to create and develop this involuntary cooperation among the people whom you supervise. For, no matter how powerful a combination of money, machines, and materials a company may have, this is a dead and sterile thing without a team of willing, thinking, and articulate people to guide it.

The following 21 points are presented as indicative of the exemplary basic relationship that should exist between supervisor and employee:

1. Each person wants to be liked and respected by his fellow employee and wants to be treated with consideration and respect by his superior.
2. The most competent employee will make an error. However, in a unit where good relations exist between the supervisor and his employees, tenseness and fear do not exist. Thus, errors are not hidden or covered up, and the efficiency of a unit is not impaired.

3. Subordinates resent rules, regulations, or orders that are unreasonable or unexplained.
4. Subordinates are quick to resent unfairness, harshness, injustices, and favoritism.
5. An employee will accept responsibility if he knows that he will be complimented for a job well done, and not too harshly chastised for failure; that his supervisor will check the cause of the failure, and, if it was the supervisor's fault, he will assume the blame therefore. If it was the employee's fault, his supervisor will explain the correct method or means of handling the responsibility.
6. An employee wants to receive credit for a suggestion he has made, that is used. If a suggestion cannot be used, the employee is entitled to an explanation. The supervisor should not say "no" and close the subject.
7. Fear and worry slow up a worker's ability. Poor working environment can impair his physical and mental health. A good supervisor avoids forceful methods, threats, and arguments to get a job done.
8. A forceful supervisor is able to train his employees individually and as a team, and is able to motivate them in the proper channels.
9. A mature supervisor is able to properly evaluate his subordinates and to keep them happy and satisfied.
10. A sensitive supervisor will never patronize his subordinates.
11. A worthy supervisor will respect his employees' confidences.
12. Definite and clear-cut responsibilities should be assigned to each executive.
13. Responsibility should always be coupled with corresponding authority.
14. No change should be made in the scope or responsibilities of a position without a definite understanding to that effect on the part of all persons concerned.
15. No executive or employee, occupying a single position in the organization, should be subject to definite orders from more than one source.
16. Orders should never be given to subordinates over the head of a responsible executive. Rather than do this, the officer in question should be supplanted.
17. Criticisms of subordinates should, whoever possible, be made privately, and in no case should a subordinate be criticized in the presence of executives or employees of equal or lower rank.
18. No dispute or difference between executives or employees as to authority or responsibilities should be considered too trivial for prompt and careful adjudication.
19. Promotions, wage changes, and disciplinary action should always be approved by the executive immediately superior to the one directly responsible.
20. No executive or employee should ever be required, or expected, to be at the same time an assistant to, and critic of, another.
21. Any executive whose work is subject to regular inspection should, wherever practicable, be given the assistance and facilities necessary to enable him to maintain an independent check of the quality of his work.

MINI-TEXT IN SUPERVISION, ADMINISTRATION, MANAGEMENT, AND ORGANIZATION

I. Brief Highlights

Listed concisely and sequentially are major headings and important data in the field for quick recall and review.

A. Levels of Management
   Any organization of some size has several levels of management. In terms of a ladder, the levels are:

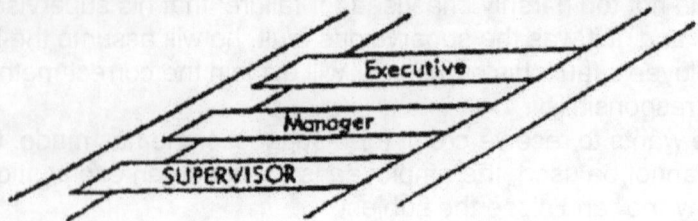

   The first level is very important because it is the beginning point of management leadership.

B. What the Supervisor Must Learn
   A supervisor must learn to:
   1. Deal with people and their differences
   2. Get the job done through people
   3. Recognize the problems when they exist
   4. Overcome obstacles to good performance
   5. Evaluate the performance of people
   6. Check his own performance in terms of accomplishment

C. A Definition of Supervisor
   The term supervisor means any individual having authority, in the interests of the employer, to hire, transfer, suspend, lay-off, recall, promote, discharge, assign, reward, or discipline other employees or responsibility to direct them, or to adjust their grievances, or effectively to recommend such action, if, in connection with the foregoing, exercise of such authority is not of a merely routine or clerical nature but requires the use of independent judgment.

D. Elements of the Team Concept
   What is involved in teamwork? The component parts are:
   1. Members
   2. A leader
   3. Goals
   4. Plans
   5. Cooperation
   6. Spirit

E. Principles of Organization
   1. A team member must know what his job is.
   2. Be sure that the nature and scope of a job are understood.
   3. Authority and responsibility should be carefully spelled out.
   4. A supervisor should be permitted to make the maximum number of decisions affecting his employees.
   5. Employees should report to only one supervisor.
   6. A supervisor should direct only as many employees as he can handle effectively.
   7. An organization plan should be flexible.

8. Inspection and performance of work should be separate.
9. Organizational problems should receive immediate attention.
10. Assign work in line with ability and experience.

F. The Four Important Parts of Every Job
1. Inherent in every job is the *accountability* for results.
2. A second set of factors in every job is *responsibilities*.
3. Along with duties and responsibilities one must have the *authority* to act within certain limits without obtaining permission to proceed.
4. No job exists in a vacuum. The supervisor is surrounded by key *relationships*.

G. Principles of Delegation
Where work is delegated for the first time, the supervisor should think in terms of these questions:
1. Who is best qualified to do this?
2. Can an employee improve his abilities by doing this?
3. How long should an employee spend on this?
4. Are there any special problems for which he will need guidance?
5. How broad a delegation can I make?

H. Principles of Effective Communications
1. Determine the media.
2. To whom directed?
3. Identification and source authority.
4. Is communication understood?

I. Principles of Work Improvement
1. Most people usually do only the work which is assigned to them.
2. Workers are likely to fit assigned work into the time available to perform it.
3. A good workload usually stimulates output.
4. People usually do their best work when they know that results will be reviewed or inspected.
5. Employees usually feel that someone else is responsible for conditions of work, workplace layout, job methods, type of tools/equipment, and other such factors.
6. Employees are usually defensive about their job security.
7. Employees have natural resistance to change.
8. Employees can support or destroy a supervisor.
9. A supervisor usually earns the respect of his people through his personal example of diligence and efficiency.

J. Areas of Job Improvement
The areas of job improvement are quite numerous, but the most common ones which a supervisor can identify and utilize are:
1. Departmental layout
2. Flow of work
3. Workplace layout
4. Utilization of manpower
5. Work methods
6. Materials handling

7. Utilization
8. Motion economy

K. Seven Key Points in Making Improvements
1. Select the job to be improved
2. Study how it is being done now
3. Question the present method
4. Determine actions to be taken
5. Chart proposed method
6. Get approval and apply
7. Solicit worker participation

L. Corrective Techniques of Job Improvement
Specific Problems
1. Size of workload
2. Inability to meet schedules
3. Strain and fatigue
4. Improper use of men and skills
5. Waste, poor quality, unsafe conditions
6. Bottleneck conditions that hinder output
7. Poor utilization of equipment and machine
8. Efficiency and productivity of labor

General Improvement
1. Departmental layout
2. Flow of work
3. Work plan layout
4. Utilization of manpower
5. Work methods
6. Materials handling
7. Utilization of equipment
8. Motion economy

Corrective Techniques
1. Study with scale model
2. Flow chart study
3. Motion analysis
4. Comparison of units produced to standard allowance
5. Methods analysis
6. Flow chart and equipment study
7. Down time vs. running time
8. Motion analysis

M. A Planning Checklist
1. Objectives
2. Controls
3. Delegations
4. Communications
5. Resources
6. Manpower

7. Equipment
8. Supplies and materials
9. Utilization of time
10. Safety
11. Money
12. Work
13. Timing of improvements

N. Five Characteristics of Good Directions
In order to get results, directions must be:
1. Possible of accomplishment
2. Agreeable with worker interests
3. Related to mission
4. Planned and complete
5. Unmistakably clear

O. Types of Directions
1. Demands or direct orders
2. Requests
3. Suggestion or implication
4. volunteering

P. Controls
A typical listing of the overall areas in which the supervisor should establish controls might be:
1. Manpower
2. Materials
3. Quality of work
4. Quantity of work
5. Time
6. Space
7. Money
8. Methods

Q. Orienting the New Employee
1. Prepare for him
2. Welcome the new employee
3. Orientation for the job
4. Follow-up

R. Checklist for Orienting New Employees   Yes   No
1. Do you appreciate the feelings of new employees
   when they first report for work?   ___   ___
2. Are you aware of the fact that the new employee must
   make a big adjustment to his job?   ___   ___
3. Have you given him good reasons for liking the job and
   the organization?   ___   ___
4. Have you prepared for his first day on the job?   ___   ___
5. Did you welcome him cordially and make him feel needed?   ___   ___

		Yes	No

6. Did you establish rapport with him so that he feels free to talk and discuss matters with you? ___ ___
7. Did you explain his job to him and his relationship to you? ___ ___
8. Does he know that his work will be evaluated periodically on a basis that is fair and objective? ___ ___
9. Did you introduce him to his fellow workers in such a way that they are likely to accept him? ___ ___
10. Does he know what employee benefits he will receive? ___ ___
11. Does he understand the importance of being on the job and what to do if he must leave his duty station? ___ ___
12. Has he been impressed with the importance of accident prevention and safe practice? ___ ___
13. Does he generally know his way around the department? ___ ___
14. Is he under the guidance of a sponsor who will teach the right way of doing things? ___ ___
15. Do you plan to follow-up so that he will continue to adjust successfully to his job? ___ ___

S. Principles of Learning
1. Motivation
2. Demonstration or explanation
3. Practice

T. Causes of Poor Performance
1. Improper training for job
2. Wrong tools
3. Inadequate directions
4. Lack of supervisory follow-up
5. Poor communications
6. Lack of standards of performance
7. Wrong work habits
8. Low morale
9. Other

U. Four Major Steps in On-The-Job Instruction
1. Prepare the worker
2. Present the operation
3. Tryout performance
4. Follow-up

V. Employees Want Five Things
1. Security
2. Opportunity
3. Recognition
4. Inclusion
5. Expression

W. Some Don'ts in Regard to Praise
1. Don't praise a person for something he hasn't done.
2. Don't praise a person unless you can be sincere.
3. Don't be sparing in praise just because your superior withholds it from you.
4. Don't let too much time elapse between good performance and recognition of it

X. How to Gain Your Workers' Confidence
Methods of developing confidence include such things as:
1. Knowing the interests, habits, hobbies of employees
2. Admitting your own inadequacies
3. Sharing and telling of confidence in others
4. Supporting people when they are in trouble
5. Delegating matters that can be well handled
6. Being frank and straightforward about problems and working conditions
7. Encouraging others to bring their problems to you
8. Taking action on problems which impede worker progress

Y. Sources of Employee Problems
On-the-job causes might be such things as:
1. A feeling that favoritism is exercised in assignments
2. Assignment of overtime
3. An undue amount of supervision
4. Changing methods or systems
5. Stealing of ideas or trade secrets
6. Lack of interest in job
7. Threat of reduction in force
8. Ignorance or lack of communications
9. Poor equipment
10. Lack of knowing how supervisor feels toward employee
11. Shift assignments

Off-the-job problems might have to do with:
1. Health
2. Finances
3. Housing
4. Family

Z. The Supervisor's Key to Discipline
There are several key points about discipline which the supervisor should keep in mind:
1. Job discipline is one of the disciplines of life and is directed by the supervisor.
2. It is more important to correct an employee fault than to fix blame for it.
3. Employee performance is affected by problems both on the job and off.
4. Sudden or abrupt changes in behavior can be indications of important employee problems.
5. Problems should be dealt with as soon as possible after they are identified.
6. The attitude of the supervisor may have more to do with solving problems than the techniques of problem solving.
7. Correction of employee behavior should be resorted to only after the supervisor is sure that training or counseling will not be helpful.

8. Be sure to document your disciplinary actions.
9. Make sure that you are disciplining on the basis of facts rather than personal feelings.
10. Take each disciplinary step in order, being careful not to make snap judgments, or decisions based on impatience.

AA. Five Important Processes of Management
1. Planning
2. Organizing
3. Scheduling
4. Controlling
5. Motivating

BB. When the Supervisor Fails to Plan
1. Supervisor creates impression of not knowing his job
2. May lead to excessive overtime
3. Job runs itself—supervisor lacks control
4. Deadlines and appointments missed
5. Parts of the work go undone
6. Work interrupted by emergencies
7. Sets a bad example
8. Uneven workload creates peaks and valleys
9. Too much time on minor details at expense of more important tasks

CC. Fourteen General Principles of Management
1. Division of work
2. Authority and responsibility
3. Discipline
4. Unity of command
5. Unity of direction
6. Subordination of individual interest to general interest
7. Remuneration of personnel
8. Centralization
9. Scalar chain
10. Order
11. Equity
12. Stability of tenure of personnel
13. Initiative
14. Esprit de corps

DD. Change

Bringing about change is perhaps attempted more often, and yet less well understood, than anything else the supervisor does. How do people generally react to change? (People tend to resist change that is imposed upon them by other individuals or circumstances.

Change is characteristic of every situation. It is a part of every real endeavor where the efforts of people are concerned.

1. Why do people resist change?
   People may resist change because of:
   a. Fear of the unknown
   b. Implied criticism
   c. Unpleasant experiences in the past
   d. Fear of loss of status
   e. Threat to the ego
   f. Fear of loss of economic stability

2. How can we best overcome the resistance to change?
   In initiating change, take these steps:
   a. Get ready to sell
   b. Identify sources of help
   c. Anticipate objections
   d. Sell benefits
   e. Listen in depth
   f. Follow up

II. Brief Topical Summaries

   A. Who/What is the Supervisor?
      1. The supervisor is often called the "highest level employee and the lowest level manager."
      2. A supervisor is a member of both management and the work group. He acts as a bridge between the two.
      3. Most problems in supervision are in the area of human relations, or people problems.
      4. Employees expect: Respect, opportunity to learn and to advance, and a sense of belonging, and so forth.
      5. Supervisors are responsible for directing people and organizing work. Planning is of paramount importance.
      6. A position description is a set of duties and responsibilities inherent to a given position.
      7. It is important to keep the position description up-to-date and to provide each employee with his own copy.

   B. The Sociology of Work
      1. People are alike in many ways; however, each individual is unique.
      2. The supervisor is challenged in getting to know employee differences. Acquiring skills in evaluating individuals is an asset.
      3. Maintaining meaningful working relationships in the organization is of great importance.
      4. The supervisor has an obligation to help individuals to develop to their fullest potential.
      5. Job rotation on a planned basis helps to build versatility and to maintain interest and enthusiasm in work groups.
      6. Cross training (job rotation) provides backup skills.

7. The supervisor can help reduce tension by maintaining a sense of humor, providing guidance to employees, and by making reasonable and timely decisions. Employees respond favorably to working under reasonably predictable circumstances.
8. Change is characteristic of all managerial behavior. The supervisor must adjust to changes in procedures, new methods, technological changes, and to a number of new and sometimes challenging situations.
9. To overcome the natural tendency for people to resist change, the supervisor should become more skillful in initiating change.

C. Principles and Practices of Supervision
1. Employees should be required to answer to only one superior.
2. A supervisor can effectively direct only a limited number of employees, depending upon the complexity, variety, and proximity of the jobs involved.
3. The organizational chart presents the organization in graphic form. It reflects lines of authority and responsibility as well as interrelationships of units within the organization.
4. Distribution of work can be improved through an analysis using the "Work Distribution Chart."
5. The "Work Distribution Chart" reflects the division of work within a unit in understandable form.
6. When related tasks are given to an employee, he has a better chance of increasing his skills through training.
7. The individual who is given the responsibility for tasks must also be given the appropriate authority to insure adequate results.
8. The supervisor should delegate repetitive, routine work. Preparation of recurring reports, maintaining leave and attendance records are some examples.
9. Good discipline is essential to good task performance. Discipline is reflected in the actions of employees on the job in the absence of supervision.
10. Disciplinary action may have to be taken when the positive aspects of discipline have failed. Reprimand, warning, and suspension are examples of disciplinary action.
11. If a situation calls for a reprimand, be sure it is deserved and remember it is to be done in private.

D. Dynamic Leadership
1. A style is a personal method or manner of exerting influence.
2. Authoritarian leaders often see themselves as the source of power and authority.
3. The democratic leader often perceives the group as the source of authority and power.
4. Supervisors tend to do better when using the pattern of leadership that is most natural for them.
5. Social scientists suggest that the effective supervisor use the leadership style that best fits the problem or circumstances involved.
6. All four styles—telling, selling, consulting, joining—have their place. Using one does not preclude using the other at another time.

7. The theory X point of view assumes that the average person dislikes work, will avoid it whenever possible, and must be coerced to achieve organizational objectives.
8. The theory Y point of view assumes that the average person considers work to be a natural as play, and, when the individual is committed, he requires little supervision or direction to accomplish desired objectives.
9. The leader's basic assumptions concerning human behavior and human nature affect his actions, decisions, and other managerial practices.
10. Dissatisfaction among employees is often present, but difficult to isolate. The supervisor should seek to weaken dissatisfaction by keeping promises, being sincere and considerate, keeping employees informed, and so forth.
11. Constructive suggestions should be encouraged during the natural progress of the work.

E. Processes for Solving Problems
1. People find their daily tasks more meaningful and satisfying when they can improve them.
2. The causes of problems, or the key factors, are often hidden in the background. Ability to solve problems often involves the ability to isolate them from their backgrounds. There is some substance to the cliché that some persons "can't see the forest for the trees."
3. New procedures are often developed from old ones. Problems should be broken down into manageable parts. New ideas can be adapted from old one.
4. People think differently in problem-solving situations. Using a logical, patterned approach is often useful. One approach found to be useful includes these steps:
   a. Define the problem
   b. Establish objectives
   c. Get the facts
   d. Weigh and decide
   e. Take action
   f. Evaluate action

F. Training for Results
1. Participants respond best when they feel training is important to them.
2. The supervisor has responsibility for the training and development of those who report to him.
3. When training is delegated to others, great care must be exercised to insure the trainer has knowledge, aptitude, and interest for his work as a trainer.
4. Training (learning) of some type goes on continually. The most successful supervisor makes certain the learning contributes in a productive manner to operational goals.
5. New employees are particularly susceptible to training. Older employees facing new job situations require specific training, as well as having need for development and growth opportunities.
6. Training needs require continuous monitoring.
7. The training officer of an agency is a professional with a responsibility to assist supervisors in solving training problems.

8. Many of the self-development steps important to the supervisor's own growth are equally important to the development of peers and subordinates. Knowledge of these is important when the supervisor consults with others on development and growth opportunities.

G. Health, Safety, and Accident Prevention
1. Management-minded supervisors take appropriate measures to assist employees in maintaining health and in assuring safe practices in the work environment.
2. Effective safety training and practices help to avoid injury and accidents.
3. Safety should be a management goal. All infractions of safety which are observed should be corrected without exception.
4. Employees' safety attitude, training and instruction, provision of safe tools and equipment, supervision, and leadership are considered highly important factors which contribute to safety and which can be influenced directly by supervisors.
5. When accidents do occur, they should be investigated promptly for very important reasons, including the fact that information which is gained can be used to prevent accidents in the future.

H. Equal Employment Opportunity
1. The supervisor should endeavor to treat all employees fairly, without regard to religion, race, sex, or national origin.
2. Groups tend to reflect the attitude of the leader. Prejudice can be detected even in very subtle form. Supervisors must strive to create a feeling of mutual respect and confidence in every employee.
3. Complete utilization of all human resources is a national goal. Equitable consideration should be accorded women in the work force, minority-group members, the physically and mentally handicapped, and the older employee. The important question is: "Who can do the job?"
4. Training opportunities, recognition for performance, overtime assignments, promotional opportunities, and all other personnel actions are to be handled on an equitable basis.

I. Improving Communications
1. Communications is achieving understanding between the sender and the receiver of a message. It also means sharing information—the creation of understanding.
2. Communication is basic to all human activity. Words are means of conveying meanings; however, real meanings are in people.
3. There are very practical differences in the effectiveness of one-way, impersonal, and two-way communications. Words spoken face-to-face are better understood. Telephone conversations are effective, but lack the rapport of person-to-person exchanges. The whole person communicates.
4. Cooperation and communication in an organization go hand in hand. When there is a mutual respect between people, spelling out rules and procedures for communicating is unnecessary.
5. There are several barriers to effective communications. These include failure to listen with respect and understanding, lack of skill in feedback, and misinterpreting the meanings of words used by the speaker. It is also common

practice to listen to what we want to hear, and tune out things we do not want to hear.
6. Communication is management's chief problem. The supervisor should accept the challenge to communicate more effectively and to improve interagency and intra-agency communications.
7. The supervisor may often plan for and conduct meetings. The planning phase is critical and may determine the success or the failure of a meeting.
8. Speaking before groups usually requires extra effort. Stage fright may never disappear completely, but it can be controlled.

J. Self-Development
1. Every employee is responsible for his own self-development.
2. Toastmaster and toastmistress clubs offer opportunities to improve skills in oral communications.
3. Planning for one's own self-development is of vital importance. Supervisors know their own strengths and limitations better than anyone else.
4. Many opportunities are open to aid the supervisor in his developmental efforts, including job assignments; training opportunities, both governmental and non-governmental—to include universities and professional conferences and seminars.
5. Programmed instruction offers a means of studying at one's own rate.
6. Where difficulties may arise from a supervisor's being away from his work for training, he may participate in televised home study or correspondence courses to meet his self-development needs.

K. Teaching and Training
1. The Teaching Process
Teaching is encouraging and guiding the learning activities of students toward established goals. In most cases this process consists of five steps: preparation, presentation, summarization, evaluation, and application.

   a. Preparation
   Preparation is two-fold in nature; that of the supervisor and the employee. Preparation by the supervisor is absolutely essential to success. He must know what, when, where, how, and whom he will teach. Some of the factors that should be considered are:
   1) The objectives
   2) The materials needed
   3) The methods to be used
   4) Employee participation
   5) Employee interest
   6) Training aids
   7) Evaluation
   8) Summarization

   Employee preparation consists in preparing the employee to receive the material. Probably the most important single factor in the preparation of the employee is arousing and maintaining his interest. He must know the objectives of the training, why he is there, how the material can be used, and its importance to him.

b. Presentation
In presentation, have a carefully designed plan and follow it. The plan should be accurate and complete, yet flexible enough to meet situations as they arise. The method of presentation will be determined by the particular situation and objectives.

c. Summary
A summary should be made at the end of every training unit and program. In addition, there may be internal summaries depending on the nature of the material being taught. The important thing is that the trainee must always be able to understand how each part of the new material relates to the whole.

d. Application
The supervisor must arrange work so the employee will be given a chance to apply new knowledge or skills while the material is still clear in his mind and interest is high. The trainee does not really know whether he has learned the material until he has been given a chance to apply it. If the material is not applied, it loses most of its value.

e. Evaluation
The purpose of all training is to promote learning. To determine whether the training has been a success or failure, the supervisor must evaluate this learning.
In the broadest sense, evaluation includes all the devices, methods, skills, and techniques used by the supervisor to keep himself and the employees informed as to their progress toward the objectives they are pursuing. The extent to which the employee has mastered the knowledge, skills, and abilities, or changed his attitudes, as determined by the program objectives, is the extent to which instruction has succeeded or failed.
Evaluation should not be confined to the end of the lesson, day, or program but should be used continuously. We shall note later the way this relates to the rest of the teaching process.

2. Teaching Methods
A teaching method is a pattern of identifiable student and instructor activity used in presenting training material.
All supervisors are faced with the problem of deciding which method should be used at a given time.

a. Lecture
The lecture is direct oral presentation of material by the supervisor. The present trend is to place less emphasis on the trainer's activity and more on that of the trainee.

b. Discussion
Teaching by discussion or conference involves using questions and other techniques to arouse interest and focus attention upon certain areas, and by doing so creating a learning situation. This can be one of the most

valuable methods because it gives the employees an opportunity to express their ideas and pool their knowledge.

    c. Demonstration
The demonstration is used to teach how something works or how to do something. It can be used to show a principle or what the results of a series of actions will be. A well-staged demonstration is particularly effective because it shows proper methods of performance in a realistic manner.

    d. Performance
Performance is one of the most fundamental of all learning techniques or teaching methods. The trainee may be able to tell how a specific operation should be performed but he cannot be sure he knows how to perform the operation until he has done so.
As with all methods, there are certain advantages and disadvantages to each method.

    e. Which Method to Use
Moreover, there are other methods and techniques of teaching. It is difficult to use any method without other methods entering into it. In any learning situation, a combination of methods is usually more effective than any one method alone.

Finally, evaluation must be integrated into the other aspects of the teaching-learning process.

It must be used in the motivation of the trainees; it must be used to assist in developing understanding during the training; and it must be related to employee application of the results of training.

This is distinctly the role of the supervisor.